BROKEN RIBS
in EVERY PEW

Within our congregations there are
believers suffering with hurts
hidden behind praise and exaltation

BISHOP LEROY C. E. NEWMAN
& MATTIE

To order additional copies of this book, contact:
Bookwhip
1-855-339-3589
https://www.bookwhip.com

TIME MINISTRY BOOK

&

TROY 4 LIFE PRODUCTION

Time Music Group, Inc
115-11 229th Street, Cambria Heights, NY 11411
1 718 723-3716
www.timemusicgroup.net

CONTENTS

INTRODUCTION

Much of my experience in ministry has come as result of a great deal of perseverance and after many trials and test at the hand of God. Perhaps the most valuable lesson I have learned is that "the trying of our faith worketh patience," and that a great deal of the hurt that believers experience in ministry is for the testing of their faithfulness. This book will focus on the healing process, and if after having reading it you conclude that the hurt you experienced at the hand of your brothers or sisters in and out of church was one of God's ways of testing your readiness or worthiness to move to another level in ministry, this book will have served you well.

In church, know that we tend to see things differently than they really are, that is to say, we think of our brothers and sisters as being "free" when we see them praising and magnifying God; we see them under a Glory Cloud, and not in the misery that many of them are in. I wrote this book because I'm convinced that on every pew in our fellowship there are believers with hurts and miseries hidden behind their praises and the exaltations. Many believers who really love God are going home to abusive situations, condition and circumstances that lead to battery, and disrespect by their husbands, their children, other family members and/or their significant others; you name the relationship and I'll point to the possibilities of hurt.

There are so many different ways through which hurt hides itself in the church and in the lives of believer that it would take a lifetime to try and write all the books needed to cover the severity of its affect on church and society; in contrast to the reality of this dilemma, most preachers are given 30 to 45 minutes to preach and minister to a multiplicity of hurts and circumstances that occurs in the daily walk of a believer and non-believers alike. Regardless of the circumstances or the depth of their pain, it is the job of the church to minister to the wounded in our congregations.

All hurt is not physical; although there are those who may not be suffering from physically, but they may simply be in dry places in their ministries, unable to see the favor of God; they may be praying, and it seems that God has turned a deaf ear to their cries; the prophet has prophesied their victory, but they feel that they are still in the midst of the battle; they have no joy, no power, nor do they have the assurance that God cares; but in this book I assure you that no matter what you feel like, you can speak victory over your circumstances and be delivered; as the song writer notes, "speak over yourself and encourage yourself," and be delivered from the brokenness and the emptiness that dominates and fragments your life; there is a wholeness and a fulfillment of purpose that turns our visions into reality and fulfills the promises of God our your lives.

This book is to assure you that you are not alone in your struggle to please God, nor to overcome your appetite for the forbidden. You need only to look around to the right and left of yourself to see someone just like yourself. There is no formula for hurt, no state of alienation that precludes you from its devastating affect. No matter what your station in life, you are susceptible to hurt. The holiest of us must endure the pains of ministry and the sufferings of our Lord in our walk with Him. It is the badge of the believer. "If we don't suffer with Him we can't reign with Him."

ACKNOWLEDGMENTS

Let me begin by acknowledging my church family; it is through ministry that I have found favor, time and the inclination to write this book; my sons, Israel, Tramine, and Laroi (Emory) and my wife, Mattie, who shares authorship of the book, gave me an immeasurable amount of support, while at the same time contributed to the content of the text; as we thought out each area we wanted to expound upon much time was given to prayer. I must make mention of a few friends who I think made a difference in my disposition during this journey: Dr. George P. Blount and Mrs. Christine Marmol, whose friendship gave me strength when the odds were against me. Rev. Inez Lebeau, a wonderful friend, Mr. Bill Kahn who has always demonstrated genuine concern for my well being and overall health, Ms. Meyerline Benjamin whose steadfast love and appreciation for me reaches beyond just being co-workers, but friendship.

I must not overlook my appreciation for the authors of Pulpit Commentary and World Aflame Publishing for their research which made it easy to develop though and direction while writing; much of the foundational information in this text came from Pulpit Commentary. I also drew from sermons preached in my church by visiting pastors and ministers: Bishop Ronald Carter, Dr. Aretha Wilson, Prophet Andre Cook, Bishop Shelvis Green, Elder Corey Oshikoya and the list goes on. Shemika Robinson has stood by Mattie and me from the being of this project; she has become a personal adjutant for us, proofing and typing much of what we wrote. Prophetess Tonya McDowell was always available to advise us to scripture interpretation and context. It would be remiss of me to not mention Bishop Joseph Williams, an Apostle in his own rights whose friendship and leadership has been more than I can say in a few lines of text, a blessing to me, my church, and the fulfillment of my vision. Finally, let me thank Tammy Mitchell for the final proof reading and all of those who shared with us the hurt and misfortune they have experienced in their lives and ministry over the years.

FOREWORD

B orn with a broken bone, it was not until the doctor took an x-ray that the patient knew the reason for his discomfort; it didn't hurt always, only at certain times; we all know people whose miseries flair up at certain times: when it rains, when the pollen is high, when they are around certain kinds of animals or chemical. There are believers in all phases of ministry who suffer with conditions that affect their spiritual development and their personal relationships (hidden conditions stimulated by spiritual weaknesses and social immorality.) The earth is full of latent forces, concealed in the elements of nature that can help us or harm us. If we look at the structure of electricity, we will discover that it is all around us, even in us; a powerful force it is. There have been reports of spontaneous human combustion which is described as the burning of a living human's body without an apparent external source of ignition.

Sin is a disease of the soul that results in the manifestation of hurt and brokenness; sin hides within the character of man while hurt hides in man's disposition, We would never know hurt if nothing ever happened to cause it to show itself; we may compare it to the seed of a disease that lay hidden in the body beneath our pure countenance and radiant complexions; hurt hides deep in the heart of man behind the beauty of life, revealing itself only when the pressures of life forces it to do so. Only through Christ and his cross can we overcome it, for we also have in us an element of faith which the Holy Spirit calls forth so that we may walk in the hope and joy of God.

We have within us the Gospel of Jesus Christ which is the power of God unto salvation as revealed in the scripture; it sustains us when our spiritual disposition is threaten. When we are pleased with our outward life and long lasting friendships, we do not always feel the hurts that beats upon our character and temperament. Again, it brings us back to the flesh; when the flesh becomes unhappy with the direction we are taking it, it find reason to rebel (to display hurt), to find fault in others, even with itself.

We hope, after you have read this text that you will discover ways to mend your brokenness and or to help someone else find deliverance from their hopelessness. I have not written this book in a vacuum; I, myself, for many years hid my brokenness behind praise until I discovered the source of my problem. This book will focuses on the brokenness that hides in the hearts and lives of believers. The root that feeds most of humanity's problems is deeply embedded in the fabric of our society. Society forces us to be pretenders, to hide behind smiles, and to dress for success, but behind the mink coat, the late model car, and the look of success are the pains of living.

The Lord wants us to trust Him, to have faith in His word; although the beauty of our flesh is His creation, He has asked us not to put our confidence in it. The flesh is temporary; Job says it comes up in the morning and by evening it is cut down. We walk by faith and not by sight. The flesh seeks to satisfy the senses: the way we feel and look or think things to be; to satisfy the flesh is to deny the fulfillment of God's Divine purpose in our lives.

RESENTMENT

Resentment is an emotion that emanates out of hatred which is the seedbed of jealousy, one of the most dangerous forms of hate; often those who suffer from "the curse of resentment" are unaware of the hurt that emerges out of it (both physically and emotionally); they often think and feel justified by their action toward and judgment of others. Resentment is an emotion that causes one to feel angry and bitter about a matter, or because of a situation; it causes one to be unwilling to give up what he or she perceives as a "right" for wrong; this unwillingness to be falsely accused often results in an intense desire to get even.

The Jews resented the popularity of Jesus; they were jealous of His ability to inspire large numbers of people to stop and listen to His message of the Kingdom of Heaven; their resentment and jealousy gave birth to the hatred which led to His crucifixion.

We can see from the crucifixion that resentment is dangerous and can also leads to murder, as in the case of Cain, whose resentment rose out of Abel's offering of a sacrifice which was more acceptable to God than his; this resulted in Cain murdering his brother. As believers we must be careful not to allow the spirit of jealousy or envy to rise up in us and lead to the destruction of our sisters' and brothers' character nor their spiritual development. We must be careful with the words we use; emotionally loaded words can kill while word spoken with soberness can cause one to live, "Out of the mouth proceeds both life and death"

> *Death and life are in the power of the tongue: and they that love it shall eat the fruit thereof.*

Proverbs 18:21

Resentment is the mother of malice which gives birth to the conspiracy to commit sin. As we deal with resentment and revisit Mark 6:16-29, keep in mind that any promise which results in the commission of a sin, must not be kept; we must repent of such promises which is in reality, the undoing of what we have done amiss. In the case of Cain and Abel, Cain's resentment was toward God but taken out on Abel. In the case of Herod and Herodias, their resentment was directed toward John the Baptist.

Herod Antipas had done an unthinkable wrong; he had driven his wife away and eloped with Herodias, his brother Phillip's wife, this prompted a word form the Lord through John the Baptist, "It is unlawful for you to marry your brother's wife" while he is still alive and while you are still married.

> *For Herod himself had sent forth and laid hold upon John, and bound him in prison for Herodias' sake, his brother Philip's wife: for he had married her.*
>
> *For John had said unto Herod, It is not lawful for thee to have thy brother's wife.*

Mark 6:17-18

The scandal grew, fueled by the preaching of John; all the country cried "shame" for it, and reproached him for it, but John reproved him; Herod resented John's accusation; The more John preached the more Herod's resentment grew for John's preaching; but at the same time Herod showed a sort of respectful fear of John, believing that John was Elijah rose from the dead. *"He feared John, knowing that he was a just man, and holy.*" Some men have a great respect and reverence for good men, especially for good ministers, and yet they themselves are bad men. Many make great sacrifices toward Grace and the Glory of God, and yet, come short of both, and perish themselves eternally. Resentment does not blind one to the good of others, but it does makes one indifferent; Herod saw that John was a *"just and holy man"* when you are *"just"* and *"holy"* it demands adoration and respect; many are not good themselves but have respect for those who are.

It was the resentment of Herod's wife, Herodias, that set the tone of the chapter; we see it quickly turned into malice, *"she had a quarrel with him, and would have killed him,"* when she could not hush or stop his preaching or orchestrate his death herself, she conspired to have him imprisoned. Those who resent God's favor toward others will seek to limit their spiritual development or hold up their blessings, and delay the reality of their vision. They will try to imprison them behind walls of fear and doubt. But John was not to be moved by her threats or frightened by her insinuations. Some, like Herodias, display their resentment openly while others do it behind acts of piety or good will. It is evident that Herod harbored some resentment for John's preaching, but waited for a better time to get even; note, he says, *"When a convenient day comes."* I am convinced that Herod was in on the plot to behead John; he may have pretended to be surprised at the request of Salome when she asked for John's head, but I am apt to believe that the whole plot was concerted by Herodias and himself; the banquet was just a stage set for the execution.

Hidden resentment often results in conspiracy to hurt or to destroy the character of others. Murder was no mystery to Herod for he had witness his father's murder of Marianne, his wife; he also witnessed the slaughter of all male infants who could possibly be considered heir to the throne, while at the same time conspired to limit the development of the Jews during his last days as leader of the Jewish people.

3

Resentment may seem to be one of those emotions, not to be taken seriously; however, what I hoped to have done in this chapter is to make you aware of the dangers that such an emotion can poses on the believer; it is the seedbed of many other harmful emotions that can adversely affect ones Christian development.

Look at Saul who resented the anointing of David as King of Israel; he too harbored or hid his resentment for David, but as long as David did not show any desire for his office or make any effort toward fulfilling his Divine Purpose as King, Saul didn't worry about David's calling. We are all called with Divine Purpose, but the enemy does not care about our calling nor does he worry about our popularity or the publishing of our desires until we do something that will turn our Divine Purpose into reality. As long as David watched his father's sheep, wrestled with bares, killed lions, Saul's resentment laid dormant, but the moment David did something that threaten Saul's office as king the resentment was awaken and lead to efforts to stop or delay the reality of David's calling. As long as you do nothing about your calling, as long as you allow the enemy to satisfy you with crumb from the table, as long as you are happy with things the way they are, you may never experience resentment toward yourself; it won't be until you make an effort to step into your Divine Purpose that the enemy will turn his attention toward you. Resentment forms a barrier, sometimes visible and open, other times dormant and hidden, but as dangerous to our development as Christians or as just ordinary people. We must guard against developing the spirit of resentment; "*if you have an aught against your brother, go to such a one*". If you have wronged your brother, first be reconciled with him. David said, "*If I regard iniquity in my heart, the Lord will not hear me.*" We cannot present gifts or service to the Lord if our hearts are filled with ought or wrong. Brotherly love is essential to Godly favor and acceptance. Worship cannot be acceptable to God, when offered by men who are not in brotherly love. We must put our minds and hearts right toward our brothers, or God will never accept it as right toward him. *"If we love not our brother whom we have seen, how can we love God whom we have not seen?" "If we love God, we should love our brother also".*

The responsibility of maintaining brotherhood rest with the Christian; however aggravating our brother may be we, as Christians, are bound to keep up the brotherhood. We cannot say, *"My brother will be reconciled with me"*; He must be, and we as Christians, cannot rest until he is. Pulpit commentary (Matthews Page 225)

The sin offering was first offered, then the burnt offering because until guilt is removed no acceptable service can be performed. We are to counter resentment with compassion. Webster's Collegiate Dictionary has defined compassion as "Sympathetic consciousness of another's distress together with a desire to alleviate it." Certainly, this definition characterizes the very nature of God in His dealings with mankind and should reflect our character when dealing with those who have displayed some form of resentment toward us. As living epistles, we are the essence of God's Word which He sent into the world through the preaching of prophets and later through His own incarnation. As we reflect the character of God in our walk with Him, we exemplify the purpose of the Church to present for believers the opportunity to take advantage of God's compassion for the world to be at peace and fruitful.

Resentment drives us to be revengeful, but God's love and Grace leads us to be compassionate toward each other. The study of Israel's history reveals an occasion where enmity between Israel and Judah resulted in Israel capturing a large number of prisoners from Judah. (See II Chronicles 28:15) These prisoners were thirsty and weary and would have been treated harshly had it not been for the prophet Obed, who declared that God would not be pleased with such harshness. Consequently Israel gave the captives clothing, food, and drink. In other words, those who show resentment toward us must be treated with compassion and love.

Church Alive, Page 50 winter 2008, World Aflame Pub.

Resentment makes one bitter; bitterness is an emotion that brings devastation in our lives; I reviewed a sermon by Eugene P. Harder, B.Th., the author of "The Deadly Root of Bitterness." He focused on the emotions that stems from bitterness. I agree with the list of emotions he developed which includes the following: He begins by saying that bitterness is an attitude of sin; It is also my belief that resentment is the mother of bitterness and that it is the triggering emotion that put on display a wide range of other sins 'that accompany it: hatred, cruelty, antagonism, self-pity, un-teachable spirits (implacability), vindictiveness, the desires for revenge, and prideful ambition (arrogance). Bitterness is characterized by an unforgiving spirit, negativity, and finally, critical attitudes. I'm going to reflect upon some passages highlighted by Pastor Harder in his sermon. Let's visit Acts 8:14-24. As fore stated, God's power cannot be manifest in nor through a life that harbors the root of resentment. Must we choose between bitterness and the indwelling presence of the Holy Spirit? Yes.

The Apostle detected a spirit of bitterness hidden in the character of Simon; as we read the chapter from a literal perspective, we see greed, perhaps pride and an unholy ambition, but the apostle Paul discerned, hidden beneath the obvious, was the spirit of bitterness growing and producing its devastating fruit. Simon was a Believer; we know this because verse 13 tells us that he was. Being a baptized believer does not alienate us from the rudiments of sin; consider this: these were new born babes who had not received the gift of the Holy Ghost (verse 17), the old man had not yet been modified. We must pay particular attention to the phrase "babes in the Lord." Much of who they are is hidden; I detect sincerity in Simon but it is a carnal sincerity, developed on a carnal foundation.

Another fruit of bitterness is habitual complaining, read Job 7:1-11; it is not enough for a bitter person to keep his or her feelings to him or herself; they find great pleasure in gossip or in making their feeling known. Look at Psalm 63:1-6. When we study the effects of resentment, we discover that bitterness fragments the lives of other people.

> *See to it that no one comes short of the grace of God and that no root of bitterness springing up cause trouble, and by it many be defiled.*
>
> *Hebrews 12:15*

> *Hear my voice, O God, in my prayer: preserve my life from fear of the enemy. 2 Hide me from the secret counsel of the wicked; from the insurrection of the workers of iniquity: 3 Who whet their tongue like a sword, and bend their bows to shoot their arrows, even bitter words: 4 That they may shoot in secret at the perfect: suddenly do they shoot at him, and fear not. 5 They encourage themselves in an evil matter: they commune of laying snares privily; they say, Who shall see them? 6 They search out iniquities; they accomplish a diligent search: both the inward thought of every one of them, and the heart, is deep.*
>
> *Psalm 63:1-6*

Let's look at some of the causes of resentment and/or bitterness; it is a fact that much of what we identified in the above paragraphs is the results of life experiences. Some women are bitter because they cannot have children (I Sam 1:10); others are bitter because of the rebellion and foolishness of their children (Proverbs 17:25.) In ministry, many reject chastisement and respond negatively to Divine Discipline. We react to life in accordance to "truth the way we believe it to be," right or wrong. We must understand that God hates resentment and bitterness; first and foremost, He has made a way of escape for us. If we fail to rid ourselves of these devastating emotions, we open the door to Idolatry. When

Peter told Simon of Samaria that he was, "In a gall of bitterness, and in the bonds of iniquity," that represented a serious problem. Iniquity in the New Testament means lawlessness. Pastor Harder called this, "a startling revelation" You must read Pastor Harder sermon, I "googled it......" As devastating as these emotions are God has made provisions for our deliverance from them.

> *If we say that we have no sin, we deceive ourselves, and the truth is not in us. ²If we confess our sins, he isfaithful and just to forgive us our sins, and to cleanse us from all unrighteousness. ¹⁰If we say that we have not sinned, we make him a liar, and his word is not in us.*
>
> *I John 1:9*

I asked Pastor Beth Thompson to make a comment of resentment, this is what she had to say, "I see resentment affecting the unity in ministry; where, instead of bonding and forming spiritual alliances, division is birthed for a number of reasons: 1. from the promotion or elevation of another believer, 2. because of God bestowing blessing on someone else.

Resentment in ministry emerges out of the seeds of jealousy and hindrance that have been sown and lay dormant until someone other than themselves show sings of growth and development. If one allows resentment to take root in his or her ministry, every element of that ministry's leadership will be stunted or undersized and no one will be inspired to commit to the growth and development of its vision. Resentment acts as an agent of diversion and separation while at the same time separates us from the substance of whole picture to keep the vision from becoming reality.

I leave you with the words of Pastor Harder, Page 2, paragraph V: You have two clear choices, you can choose bitterness which is lawlessness and idolatry, and risk losing everything you hold near and dear, or you can choose the Holy Spirit and its positive power which you need for daily deliverance and the fulfillment of your Divine Purpose. The choices are yours, but remember it is possible to exhales time, reach your destiny and never step into your purpose; all because of resentment and bitterness.

SUFFERING

S uffering is not the curse of a few believers; it is the badge of every believer, regardless of his or her station or calling. "If we don't suffer with Him we cannot reign with Him." We suffer physically, mentally, socially, and, economically, in our families, even in our churches. The scripture says

> *"We are troubled on every side, yet not distressed; we are perplexed, but not in despair; persecuted, but not forsaken; cast down, but not destroyed;....."*

> *2 Corinthians 4:8-9*

The apostles were great sufferers, yet they met with wonderful support. As Believers we may be forsaken by our friends, and persecuted by our enemies; but God will never leave us nor forsake us. There may be fears within our hearts and physical challenges that come from without; yet we are not destroyed. We must see our sufferings as the apostles saw their sufferings, as a counterpart of the suffering of Christ, that people might see the power of His resurrection in us. We are living epistles.

> *The righteous cry, and the LORD heareth and delivereth them out of all their troubles. The LORD is nigh unto them that are of a broken heart; and saveth such as be of a contrite spirit. Many are the afflictions of the righteous: but the LORD delivereth him out of them all.*

> *Psalms 34:17*

Knowing this that the trying of your faith worketh patience.

James 1:3.

We are also admonished to *"count it all as joy when we enter into divers temptations."* Remember this, David concludes, by assuring us that *"the Lord delivereth him out of them all."* The next time you are in church, just look around and you will see other believers who are going through or who have gone through just as you have. We are not alone in the trying of our faith; it is the duty of every believer to be tried.

Whether we suffer mentally or physically, socially or spiritually; whether the encounter comes from a friend or an enemy or from within ones own family, it can not be compared to the joy which the Lord has reserved for those who endure hardness as good soldiers. Paul writes,

> *For I reckon that the sufferings of this present time are not worthy to be compared with the glory which shall be revealed in us.*
>
> *Romans 8:18*

James writes to the Church, not to the ungodly Jews who were the source of the oppression and suffering which newly converted Jews experienced. He exhorts the Church to be patient because the Lord's return to deliver it was imminent. Waiting characterizes a large part of the Believer's duty; patience is not a mere segment of the Christian character, it is a spirit which pervade or encompasses every fiber of it. To wait upon the Lord is a frequent cry in the scripture. We show our faith, not only by our works but also when we endure; our patience must co-exist along with our suffering. Let's not forget what Paul says,

> *Therefore being justified by faith, we have peace with God through our Lord Jesus Christ: By whom also we have access by faith into this grace wherein we stand, and rejoice in hope of the glory of God. And not only so, but we glory in tribulations*

also: knowing that tribulation worketh patience; And patience, experience; and experience, hope: And hope maketh not ashamed; because the love of God is shed abroad in our hearts by the Holy Ghost which is given unto us.

Romans 5:1-5

One of the reoccurring themes in the Bible is the suffering of the believers as individuals and as a group. Individually we are almost immediately introduced to "Able" who suffered the ultimate death at the hands of his brother; David said that he could understand it when the suffering comes from without, but when it comes from ones own household, it seems unbearable. We don't only suffer at the hands of our natural families, but we also suffer spiritually at the hands of sisters and brothers in the church; Paul speaks of "spiritual weaknesses in high places;" it may come from the pew and/or even form the pulpit; it may be subtle or abrasive; nevertheless, we are admonished to be patient, to endure hardness, trust God, and wait.

Abraham suffered a different challenge, his suffering was both physical and mental; he was asked to leave family; this was not always easy to do because family was the first priority of society. He was promised an unimaginable blessing; the father of many people, then many nations; the wait, given his physical ability and age, made it seemingly an un-accomplishable reality; he must have been under much mental stress, knowing that his physical ability to bear children was decreasing with the passing of each day. We must keep in mind that "blessings delayed are not blessings denied." "Wait on the Lord, be of good courage."

Israel suffered as a nation: bondage in Egypt, 40 years in the wilderness, oppress by its neighbors and placed in captivity; even today she is unaccepted by many and thought of as not to have the right to exist, but as believers, we can still hear the cry of Biblical writers echoing throughout the ages, "Wait on the Lord, Wait, I say on the Lord."

Why then, must the righteous suffer or should I say, "why must any suffer." If God is the master of every circumstance, why can't God remove suffering from among us or at least from the path of the believer? In addition to whether suffering can be elevated, there is the question of what really constitutes suffering, is it physical hurt only or can it be mental, emotional, social, economical, etc. There is a large array of the different types of sufferings that we experience as believers, but they are no different from that of the whole of humanity. Suffering is the instrument of God; he uses it to force us to move in the direction he wants us to go or to discipline us for not choosing to do what he has divinely purposed for us to do.

Let me try to deal with the question of "can God elevate suffering;" He can because He is God, but to do so would remove from humanity the option of "free will," the liberty to chose right over wrong. Suffering is one of the by products of evil or sin and disobedience. If God stops one evil he must stop all evils which include evil thinking. A world without evil would be a utopia; a utopian society is a society where there are no evils, no crime, no poverty, no civil or social disobedience, no religious ill moralities; a perfect world, heaven.

As difficult as this subject is to deal with in relation with God's use of suffering, we accept the fact that God uses one form of suffering to create a path for us around a more severe from of suffering. We find it difficult to understand why God allows evil to exist, but when we come to understand that the key component of God's Redemption Plan of Salvation was evil, or I should say, the key instrument that made our salvation possible, was evil, we then see the resentment of the Jews, the jealousy of the Sanhedrin, and the envy of the people all lead to Jesus' crucifixion and ultimately our salvation.

The irony of not enduring hardness as a good soldier is that eventually, you will have to face that challenge again. Running away from a test simply means that you will have to take it again. Daniel was delivered out of the lions' den, the Hebrew Boys were delivered from the fiery furnace, and David delivered the lamb out of the paws of the lion and the bare.

> *Many are the afflictions of the righteous: but the LORD delivereth him out of them all.*

> Ps 34:19

There are trial that are designed to make us better; they may seem bitter and untimely; it may seem easier to avoid them rather than to face them, but keep in mind that the elevation and promotion for many of God's leaders came only after their lions' den experience. Moses ran away from his Egyptian encounter only to face it 40 years later. I could go on highlighting event after event where Biblical characters had to face their challenges before elevation; however, it would be remised of me to over look the reality of the flesh and the role it plays in our suffering. The righteous suffer afflictions because they are "imperfectly righteous." Although we strive for perfection, it is a process of purging, purifying, and chastening to rid us of the impurities and defilement of sin which clings to us in such a way in which we are never wholly freed while we continue in the flesh. Acts 14:22 tell us *"We must through much tribulation enter into the Kingdom of God."* Hebrews 2:10 tells us that *salvation is made perfect through suffering.*

Many of those who suffer often feel that their suffering is God's ways of chastising them or that He has forsaking them, but we must keep in mind that God's chastisement is meant to make us better; God may at some point in our ministry use our enemy to chasten us, but no matter how great the chastening, He has promise "never to forsake us;" Jeremiah 51 tells us how God used the Chaldeans in Babylon to chastise Israel, but He never turned His back on her. Israel, at this time in her history was a down-trodden, sinful remnant of God's people, who had broken every engagement of His covenant, but He still laid claim to her as His own, and care for her. God has entered into a covenant with us, members of the Church, and even though we fail to live up to our part of the agreement, He will not withdrew His love from us. The purpose of His love is never laid aside. God created a plan of salvation while we were yet sinner, and though hidden from man, His Divine love, works continually toward us. Even though we fail Him and disobey Him, we must not mistake His chastening as being forsaken; "all things work together for the good of them that love God," "though He slay me, yet will I trust Him (Job 13:15)." Israel looked forsaken; she was exiled, into captivity and under the asserted judgment of God. Man has always accepted the appearance of thing as God's favor or as his judgment, too often have we forgotten that God's present may be manifested in many ways; outward prosperity is not what signifies that God is satisfied with us, nor is chastisement or suffering an indication that He has forsaken us. Man, because of his prolonged suffering sometimes forsake God, and lean to his own understanding. We have in the midst of the storm, turned to our own solutions to rid ourselves of the trials and misfortunes we face. Great suffers become great leaders. Suffering forces us to look beyond the physical and discern God's Divine Purpose for us.

Let me share with you a store told to me by one of my congregants about her personal challenge with suffering; hidden from the knowledge of everyone except her immediate family she endured this challenge alone. As pastors we sometimes are not able to discern the spiritual challenges of some members, while they chose to endure their challenges by themselves. This member of the church who still attends along with her daughter and her family suffered much hardship and abuse at the hands of her husband. The reason I feel that you will be blessed or encouraged by this story is, all the time I had known her and visited with her and her family, I never could have imagined the abuse she share with me 13 years after her husband was called home by God. When we hear someone say, "I don't look like what I've been through," in this case it is a true saying. She began by share with me her current economic situation; she was thrown into this situation because her husband hated and resented her because she loved her physically handicapped son, and because she refuge to put him away into a home for the mentally retarded. She said that he, her husband, constantly said to her that she loved her son more than she love him, and because of this jealousy he abused her daily. She said that she never stopped doing the things that a wife should do; she even prepared his meals and bath water daily, and yet he threatened her life constantly; the resentment for her loving their son was so great that he told her that he was not going leave her any of his pension which he had earned from working for the city of those years to her; she thought that he was joking; she knew that he was and that she had experienced his abuse almost daily; she never imagined that he would really do such a thing; apart from the physical and mental abuse there were threats against her life; he was a hunter and had high powered riffles which he used to further intimidate her; he said that he could be four or five block away and kill her and know one would ever know who did it.

As fellow laborers, we never know what our brothers and sisters are going through; we sometime miss judge the sincerity of their worship by measuring it according to our own perception of worship. As we often say, "you don't know the store behind my glory." But "the suffering of this present time cannot be compared to the joy that the Lord has prepared those who are the called...." I pray that none of you suffer the sufferings of this present time, but if you do, remember that it is the badge of the believer; if we don't suffer we can't reign with Him.

FALLOW GROUND
WILL PRODUCE

Let me begin by creating the primes that…

> *"We all have sinned and come short of the Glory of God." "For
> I know that within me (that is in my flesh) dwelleth no good
> thing: For to will is present with me: but how to perform that
> which is good I find not,"*
>
> Romans 7:18.

My parents were farmers; I didn't understand it then, but every so often they would not plant a certain section of land. The ground would be allowed to lay fallow; it would be plowed but left unseeded and unattended; in other fields the ground would be left unplowed; uncultivated. Jeremiah, in chapter 4, makes reference to "fallow ground," ground unattended, uncultivated, unproved for a season. Many of those who suffer in ministry suffer from generational hurts and are victims because they are not "living epistles" but merely "practicing religion;" they are victims because false prophets, who profess to be believers but were nothing more than wolves in sheep clothing, took advantage of their commitment to service. We are warned to beware of false prophets; they are often hidden among the true believers waiting for the opportunity to take advantage of the believers' commitment to use it for their own good. A person who once professed belief in the doctrine of

Jesus Christ but now fails to manifest Him, could be considered "fruit laying fallow;" perhaps this lack of commitment was because of a divorce or separation, or death, imprisonment, or it may be because someone just matured or went away to college, or just began to associate with new friends; there are hundreds of reasons why individuals may become less involved in fellowship and worship than they once were. Jeremiah called this the "backsliding of the nation;" however, a backslidden life style is only one way that signifies that a believer has become separated from God and need someone or something to turn its life around.

There are other reasons why one may not be a believer, consider this: it may be that an individual was never exposed to any Christian values which connects one to Christ through faith and Divine purpose, or it could be that what exposure there was, was through one of the many Christian cults that propagate half-truths about living a set apart life for Christ; there is also a bigger picture, in which we can see the lack of man's devotion to God; we can see it in the whole of humanity, in the character and disposition of the nation, in the attitudes and reactions of the people; in individuals who are not influence by spiritual values. I would go as far as to say that we, the Church as a whole, have allowed uncultivated Christian characters to invade our cultivated field of faith and sow seed of tare: The removal of prayer from our schools is fruit from uncultivated or infertile ground. However, fallow dose not always mean infertile; I shall deal with this subject later as we go on; leave a field (a soul, a life, a mind) unattended, and see if something is bound to grow; in a broader sense, it is humanity that's not under the influence of God. Fallow ground is comparatively, fruitless; but not utterly fruitless; as fore stated, even the bramble brush bears its wholesome fruit; this is not to say that nothing good can come out of barren fields; in the midst of the desert the cactus blossoms; good thoughts and good deeds have sprung out heathen nation and irreligious people. God's spirit has not wholly departed from any man; but when we compare the fruit of the Believer with that of the unbeliever, the crop of the latter is small and more easily perished. The highest thought, the purest morality, the noblest effort, the largest charity are only to be found where spiritual life is cultivated by worship, instruction, and discipline.

The heart will produce, if we plant no flower in our garden, the soil will not remain unoccupied. Whether from their peers, their teachers, neighbors, friends, or the man down the street, your children will learn. Dropped by birds or carried by the wind, in some way seeds will find their way into their lives and spring up. Some may think of fallow ground as a desert but it is not; it is a wilderness. If we do not plant good seeds in the heart, it will produce a crop of evil. The heart cannot endure a void; if it is not filled with pure thoughts, it will indulge in unholy imagination; if it is not active in doing good, it will be delighted in doing harm. Just as you develop your Christian character to produce fruit in cultivated fields, in the same proportion evil will produce weed in uncultivated fields; the more fertile the soil, the more abundant the crop or weeds.

The heart is filled with the rudiments of the flesh: hatreds, jealousy, envies, hurts that have been passed down from one generation to the next; seeds of animosity and misfortune; no matter how much good we pour into it, the good will only be choked by the evil that the flesh nurtures; throw a basket of wheat into an uncultivated field and the weeds will choke it (Matt. 13:7). We must first uproot the fruit of the flesh from the heart before a new character can be developed or take root and produce good fruit. Man must first repent before he can receive the seeds of eternal life. If the heart is hard, it will not receive the seeds of life; fallow ground must be cultivated, prepared. If the heart is preoccupied the truth will soon be forgotten. The heart must be cleared of weeds and softened to give the seeds of righteousness the opportunity to grow.

Those who suffer from broken ribs or who display hidden anxieties with outbursts of anger must come to understand the importance of breaking up fallow ground. Think of the privileges wasted and opportunities for good works neglected by nurturing unholy imaginations. It is difficult to discern ones hurt while in the midst of an unholy state of being. They are too close to their own unholy state to have the right perspective of their condition or to even know that a condition exists. Sometimes our disposition looks good and our character appears acceptable because our hurts, our passions, our self-interest, and the prejudices that pervert our judgments are hidden within the whole of our character, and reveals themselves only at times when they feel threatened; like the seeds of tare carried by the wind and find their way into the fallow ground where they wait for the opportune season to sprout.

If it is impossible for a soul to be save while clinging to sin, it is also impossible for one to reap the full benefits of grace while suffering from hidden curses of pass generations. Jeremiah in his disclosure of the fallow ground also talked about the chaos which results from sin. The root of much of what we see as generational curses is sin. Every step in sin is a step downward or backwards. One day's sin can undo the work of years in a soul's progress. Sin destroys ones commitment to vision and purpose while at the same time reduces ones spiritual life to chaos. Fasting and prayer are the chief weapons that secure our salvation; they are the strongest ties we have in our relationship with God; without them we become nothing at all. Sin is a solvent that destroys one trust in God.

Now let us revisit Matthews 13:7; Jesus spoke to the multitude in a parable: This is the first time the disciples heard Jesus use parable to reveal a hidden truth. They seemed shocked at the change in Jesus' method of teaching. Perhaps because the disciples were more advanced in religious knowledge than the multitude, they thought because they understood the mysteries of the Kingdom of God that the multitude should also understand. The truth of the Kingdom of God is a mystery, unintelligible, and incredible to the worldly and the unconverted; hidden from the wise and prudent of the world, but revealed to the babes in Christ. Knowledge of the Kingdom of God is a gift; it is not gained through thought and study. It is given by the gift of the Holy Spirit to those who commit to the teaching of Jesus Christ.

Uncultivated lives, hear the words of truth, and yet they hear not, for they do not understand the words of truth with their level of faith. They saw Jesus, and yet they saw Him not; they saw only his outward form, and failed to perceive his Divine character. Some hurts, some blindness, some generational ills are passed down through several generations (Great Grandparents, Grandparents, Parents) there are others that are self inflicted. "Their eyes they have closed". Some hear but refuse to accept God's word as truth.

Remember, we discussed previously in this chapter that Fallow Ground takes two forms, plowed and unplowed; it is the plowed that is most deceptive. Rocky ground that has been plowed appears to be good and rich, but beneath the surface is the enemy to growth. There is just enough soil at the surface to germinate the seed but not enough to nurture it. Some fallow grounds are rich and receptive in certain areas; here and there are areas of promise, areas where the believer does well, but "a little leaven, leavens the whole lump." It is possible to be knowledgeable of the Word of God and be found wanting in character.

In this chapter we spent a lot of time describing fallow ground; what I, perhaps, fail to discuss this far is its importance or its role in the growth and development of ministry. Jesus tells us in the "great commission" to go into the world and compel men to come…., He also says, "Will a man not leave the ninety and nine, and go after the one which was lost." When we see those who have fallen outside of the arch of safety, do we see weeds in uncultivated fields, or do we see fruit among thrones. Many noble men were once seeds among thrones: broken, casted down, forsaken, abused, hurt, and tried by fire; what Jesus wants us to do is to see the value of very soul whether it be among the baptized believers or among the lost of this world: drug addicts, murderers, homeless, drunker, or in whatever state one may be found; they all are important in the plan of salvation; for without them there would be no need of it.

Named among the "who so ever will" are countless seeds that are fallen on fallow ground; we must be careful how we entertain strangers, for we may entertain an angel unaware. Had Paul been alienated from ministry, just thank what would the New Testament look like or what mysteries we would have missed. He admonished us to endure the suffering no matter what.

IDENTITY CRISIS

When a believer suffers with his or her identity, the root of the problem is centered in the way the individual sees him or herself. Self-image is the key in the development of one's identity. How you feel about yourself go a long ways in healing one from the despair of "self." Low self-esteem pushes its victims into a state of depression which prevents them from developing vision and committing and their true fulfillment in Christ. God has purposed for each of us a physical form and a level of academic stewardship; when what we look like to others become more important to us than what God has purposed for us in our lives, we live beneath our privilege. Identity cannot be found in the continuity of form or in physical character; true identity is found in our harmony with the spirit and will of God for us. If we move or have our being in reflection of our physical form or material worth we risk missing the opportunity to prospering as our souls prospers.

Form must be a reflection of spiritual development and commitment to the will of God. When the physical is obtained through temporal means and carnal intent, it will soon perish, because there is no spiritual or moral value in the physical. Beauty and from are but skin deep and have only temporary promise; for they come up in the morning and they perish by noonday; *"man is born of a woman and has but a few days"(Job)*.

Don't allow yourself to be identified by your condition; when people identify you by your physical appearance they cannot appreciate the inner man who directs your path. Long after we have been delivered from our circumstance some still see us as we were, but you are no longer the woman with the six children on walfare, with no money in the bank, living in the projects. While all these things may be true, you have the power to call those things that are not as if they were; to speak life and prosperity into your own life; to see your six children as princes and princess living on Grace and the Favor of God with an inheritance of eternal life in the Kingdom of God. Don't let who other people think you are, determine your identity.

Your relationship with God is not predicated on any other believer relationship with Him. God does not require us to be like the other believers, but like other believers, we are required to be Holy and to walk worthily, to be steadfast, unmovable, and abound always in the work of the Lord. Like other believers, we are required to obey the scripture, to love, even our enemies. We are all called with different purposes; perhaps with the same gifts, but for different uses at deferent times. Our gifts become a part of our identity, and they come with different levels of anointing. It is possible for you to have the same gift and the same administration of that gift in the same service as your brother or sister in the Lord (you may sing the same song as Sister Jones in the same service) but with different levels of anointing.

When we forget whose we are and why we are call, and lean to our own understanding, we anger God. It is by His Devine Grace that He gives us a second chance or sends correction by way of trial and dismay. He may send prophets with prophesies for direction and warning; He may even appeared to us in visions and in dreams, just to give us the chance to fortify our identity with Him. A false sense of identity causes one to make excuses for neglecting to do what God has purposed; it cause one to concern oneself with what other think and expect. Low self-esteem is the seedbed for the development of an identity crisis, and makes one "other directed." Other directed people do what other people expect and not what they themselves feel. When you are other directed, you tend to use the opinions of others as an excuse for failure. "I didn't do it because….." or "I didn't want to, but she made me or told me to….," but when the Lord comes we will have to give account of our deeds, good or bad. It will all comes down to our faith or trust in God. Believing in ones self is the key to developing a positive perception of ones life. Knowing the voice of God secures ones trust in Him when stepping into purpose.

There is both glorious enjoyment and valuable influence in a man's reputation. Great men follow their reputation, while men with questionable reputations have their reputation follow them; reputation defines ones identity. A good reputation is likened to an aroma which our lives shed around us. We are always judging each other; every act of kind is appraised, but often quite unconsciously; we appear better or worse in the estimation of our neighbors according to what we do and are perceived to be; our professions, our principles, our deeds, our words, even our manners and methods, all leave impressions on the minds of others concerning ourselves. What a man thinks of us is the sum total of these impressions, and constitutes our reputation and identity.

Our character is constantly creating an atmosphere around us in which we move and live and walk freely; it is true that some good men seriously injure their reputation by some follies or even faults which might have easily have been corrected and which perhaps ought to have been avoided. As important as reputation is in defining ones identity, it is not the very best thing of all; character stands first; it is of vital consequence that we be right in the sight of God, and tried by Divine wisdom. The first and best thing is not to seem right, but to be right and wise.

Reputation is of value; it is a joy to be well-esteemed by our friends, our parents, and our children, but how much weightier or valuable are the words of the man who has been growing in honor and has a good reputation, than a man who is inexperienced and unknown or a man whose reputation has been tarnished.

The identity crisis occurs when those with whom you interact have difficulty determining how you will respond to them when they approach you with their concerns about you, or when you, yourself, fine difficulty in developing an image that is reflective of the character you perceive yourself to have. To minimize the crisis with one's self, it is necessary to trust and believe in one's abilities, and to have faith in one's successes. Success is a building block that allow you to draw upon past experiences to overcome the fear of the next challenge; look at what you were able to do, by the Grace of God, and decree that you will use the same energy to overcome the oncoming challenges and dispel the negative thoughts you have about your image. When you make a commitment to God your identity changed; you became a believer and set apart for the work of the Lord; you are no longer you own. You are now one who places one's trust in God's truth; one who takes God at His word and trusts in Him for salvation.

To merely agree to God's truth does not give you this new identify nor dose it constitute your salvation by faith, according to the Bible (John 8:31-46 Acts 8:13-24; James 2:14-26), neither is a total commitment of oneself to Jesus as Lord a form of saving faith and self-identity with Him. Such a view places too much emphasis on the act of belief, as opposed to the object of belief-Jesus Christ. This view also goes beyond the biblical perception of faith as evidence of the reception of the gift (John 4:1-42; Eph 2:8-10).

A belief that salvation rests in the finished work of Christ and Christ alone is expressed in John 3:16. Believers are those who have trusted God with their will as well as their mind (Rom 1:16; 3:22; 1 Thessalonians 1:7). Some of the classic New Testament references dealing with belief, or faith, are John 3:16,36; Acts 16:31; Rom 3:21-5:1; Gal 2:16; Eph 2:8-10; and 1 John 5:1.
Nelson's Illustrated Bible Dictionary.

SUPERFLUOUS PERCEPTION

....

The character of the believer takes president over ability and availability. We often have placed availability over ability and the faithful above the gifted, but as important as faithfulness and availability is, Paul, in speaking to Timothy places the character of the believer above both works and availability. "I would rather see a sermon than to hear one any day." What we do speak far more loudly than what we say.

The believer in manner, in conversation, and in practice must exemplify what the Grace of God is; his or her conduct and character should be a commentary on the Word of God; character speaks loudly; the function of preaching and ministering, and giving the sacraments may be performed by anyone, even a stranger, but the effectual sermon of a holy Christian life can only be demonstrated through Christian character.

The healing of a broken spirit which affects character is one of the most difficult to cure, and at most times, to detect; those who suffer with character flaws often have a lack of respect for the principles that governs ministry and for leaders who are responsible for defending those principles; they fail to understand that leaders themselves cannot trust their senses when making choices or decisions that affect the statue of Church. The senses are deceptive in that they reflex the physical or what is a matter of fact; those who seek promotion often amplify works or stewardship in order for the leadership to notice their abilities. They tend to place works above character, and when they do so they deceive themselves and have little understanding of what Paul meant when he admonished us to be living epistles. When God makes a decision through leadership His choice proves to be, *"what is that good and acceptable and perfect will of God."* God causes leaders to notice the individual's character, works and faithfulness to see whether they line up with His will. He also sends challenge to try those who are ill prepared for leadership which causes them to display unacceptable character. Challenge or failed expectations arouse or awaken hidden objectionable attributes and dispositions. When the flesh does not get what it wants it acts out of character with the Word of God; it points to stewardship and loyalty as testimony for worthiness; it hold ministry hostage by withholding its gifts and resources (it doesn't sing on the choir or pay tithes or show up for fellowship).

The flesh uses the physical in an effort to forester its will in ministry. How many times have we witnessed members of our congregations using their gifts to orchestrate elevation or promotion in ministry? How many times have they pointed to what they have done to win support for their perception of what is right? Those who suffer with a lack of respect for authority will challenge leadership and have need of a special kind of healing. *"They error because of a lack of knowledge;"* they also suffer from a lack of faith in themselves and ultimately, in leadership itself. When you understand that God is the true leader of the Church and it is He who place believers in their perspective elevations, we will be more able to accept the decisions of our leaders. The purpose that God has for one believer has nothing to do with His purpose for another; therefore, we ought not to use the character of other as a measuring stick for our worthiness.

There is nothing wrong with comparing your works with another believer, that is to say, "if God saw fit to elevate him who has been less faithful than I, He must have an elevation for me, but if He doesn't, I'll be content with my present place." The question then is, how do we orchestrate healing of such a character? Superfluous and ill prepared characters hide behind explanations and excuses; they fail to comprehend the affects of their words on the character of others. When you measure your character or worthiness by others there are only two results; one, you will see yourself better than that person or you will see that person better then you. When you question the validity of another person's elevation, you also question the worthiness of the person who God used to orchestrate the elevation, whether it is the Pastor, the Bishop, or the President of an auxiliary. The process of healing begins with being prayerful and lead by the spirit; remember, "We wrestle not against flesh and blood, but against spiritual weakness in high places." "*We error for a lack of knowledge;*" apart from fasting and praying, we must seek to heal through spirit lead education, for "*Faith comes by hearing*" (Romans 10:17.) The scripture warns in Romans 12:3 that "*we ought not think of ourselves more highly than we ought to think.*" The principles of this chapter must be practiced; renewal and consecration must not only be a testimony, but they must also fall in line with the will of God. We must not lose sight of the fact that we preach and teach not only to our congregations and the members of our communities, but also to individuals; our message is, "*to every man among you*"; we are cautioned against self-exaltation and self-praise; the early Church was very small and the number of Christians were very few; A Christian's life had both the dangers of being a Christian and the advantages of regeneration attach to it; believers were thrown together to form a society of "peculiar people," therefore self-exaltation was a necessary caution.

As besetting as temptation is, human nature cause men to think too highly of themselves. Men are prone to exaggerate their own abilities and merits while at the same time extenuate or downplay their own faults while they depreciate the gifts and desires of their neighbors. Human nature promotes selfishness, self-importance, and self-glorification. The Church reckoned pride among the seven deadly sins, but there was another reason for this Apostolic caution in the case of the early Church. In the early Church there were imparted to many Christians very remarkable and striking gifts: in some instances men who had never done anything important before were able to perform miracles never before seen within the bounders of this society of "peculiar people." these gifts were held in high esteem, and were often unduly prized and even coveted by others. The possessor of these supernatural powers: the gift of tongues and of healing may have put a person of no more than average Christian character, in danger of developing a puffed up spirit of pride. Let it be remembered that there is no gift or endowment of God's anointing which may not furnish the occasion for sinful pride. No individual is out of the reach of Satan's grip of sin, for he waits for the opportunity to present us with the occasion.

As fore-mentioned, Proverbs 6:17 list pride among the seven most deadly sin which God hates; pride is a spirit that causes one to overestimate himself and underestimate others. The superfluous nature of a man's character emanates out of that proud spirit. Pride causes one to carve out for itself a permanent place in other men's lives, yet it will not let him endure a secondary position in anyone's life, such as the giving up the right for the wrong; a proud man demands his rights, not because he will enjoy them or benefit by the exercise of them, but because they are his. He will not give them up or forego them for the sake of another. This superfluous attitude and self-assertiveness threatens the supposed rights of others, and provokes a similar spirit in ones neighbors. Romans12:3 is an important scripture to commit to memory; it may prevent the development of an egotistical personality. The sin of pride is deeply embedded in the fabric of our ministries; it can affects longstanding members of the church: pastors, deacons, missionaries, mothers, choir leaders, etc.; the sin of pride takes many forms; we often do not see it in ourselves, but we can easily see it in the character of others, perhaps because they are the ones always with a victory report or sing the loudest or sponsoring the biggest programs. One does not always set out to develop a proud spirit; sometimes it develops out of a circumstance; at other times from some members of the church think that they are in charge by some unknown criteria; W. D. Oldland says, "it my be that they have been elevated to a particular position of authority; it may be according to age, tenure, attendance, giving of time or funds, the number of responsibilities they hold in the church. Somehow an individual or individuals begin to think of themselves more highly than they ought because the enemy uses pride to trap the believer in sin. We must be careful in our estimation of ourselves; it is best that we let other people exalt us than we ourselves. Matthews tells us that the "greatest among us shall be servant and whosoever shall exalt himself shall be abased; and he that shall humble himself shall be exalted. Matt 23:11-12; Paul in 2 Corinthians 11:20 Tells us that self-exaltation causes one to suffer, while, Peter admonishes us to "Humble ourselves therefore under the mighty hand of God, that He may exalt you in due time."

We know that self-exalted people are superfluous and pretend to be more than they really are; it may have started with the development of a false perception of their character and disposition; it may have began with an innocent act of self-praise of tribute that somehow developed into self-honoring or worshipping and/or even self-glorification; regardless of its genesis, it has resulted in the deceiving of one's self. The father of pride, Satan, encourages self-exaltation which leads to the development of a carnal spirit (Martin G. Collins).

Look for a moment at what Moses had to face:

> *And they gathered themselves together against Moses and against Aaron, and said unto them, Ye take too much upon you, seeing*

all the congregation are holy, every one of them, and the LORD is among them: wherefore then lift ye up yourselves above the congregation of the LORD?

Numbers 16:3

To paraphrase, they said, "Look, who are you, Moses? You've taken this authority to yourself, but it should be shared among all the people, because we have all been called out. We are all holy before God. Why then do you exalt yourself above the congregation of the Lord?"

Notice what they say. It is quite ironic. They say, "You are taking too much authority to yourself. Everybody should have this authority" and then they accuse Moses of exalting himself: "You put yourself in this position." But were they not attempting to do the very same thing? These words would come back to haunt them very shortly (Richard T. Ritenbaugh)

Martin G. Collins writes, "<u>Satan</u> is the prime example of the self-exalted disposition, beginning with his attempt to usurp God's throne." Note the he said, "*I will*" four times in the few verses.

How you have fallen [RSSZ] from heaven, O star of the morning, son of the dawn! You have been cut down to the earth, You who have weakened the nations!

"But you said in your heart,'I will ascend to heaven; I will raise my throne above the stars of God, And I will sit on the mount of assembly In the recesses of the north.

I will ascend above the heights of the clouds; I will make myself like the Most High.'

"Nevertheless you will be thrust down to Sheol, To the recesses of the pit.

Isaiah 14:12-15

Nebuchadnezzar follows his example by his self-praise: "Is not this great Babylon, that *I* have built for a royal dwelling by *my* mighty power and for the honor of *my* majesty.

> *The king spake, and said, Is not this great Babylon, that I have built for the house of the kingdom by the might of my power, and for the honour of my majesty?*
>
> *Daniel 4:30*

The man of <u>sin</u>, the Antichrist, will be the most self-exalted human being on earth, and this same spirit of pride will drive him to exaltation.

> *Let no man deceive you by any means; for that day shall not come, except there come a falling away first, and the man of sin be revealed, the son of perdition; who opposeth and exalteth hisself above all that is called God, or that is worshipped; so that he as God sitteth in the temple of God, shewing himself that he is God.*
>
> *II Thessalonians 2:3-4*

Some have allowed the praises of others to drive them to self-exaltation; it is better to be right alone than to be wrong with a thousand. Don't be an "other directed" person; think for yourself and of yourself; there is nothing wrong with appreciating ones self for his or her own accomplishments.

FOLLY OF TRUSTING FLESH

....

"*P*ut not your trust in princes, nor in any child of man," said the Psalmist (146:3) "*for there is no help in them.*" Flesh, that is men are not always of one mind; they say what they do not mean and regret what they have promised. They find ways to escape keeping their vows or else they boldly break them with a contemptuous disregard to what others think or say.

The interest of the flesh changes quickly; what seemed to be a wise policy today, may seem foolish or even mad on tomorrow. Men sometimes make heavy sacrifices to develop an alliance or a friendship or to obtain an object of interest, but make no sacrifice to maintain it; they sigh or crave for things that they do not have and despise what they do have. The flesh can never be satisfied, it is forever wanting, uncertain, and giving in to the fickleness of man, who is naturally "*double-minded and unstable in all his ways*" *(James 1:8)*.

Physiologically, the human side of man protects the security of the mind with the best intentions in the world, but often this has proven to be insufficient. The very one to whom we turn for help often become our oppressor. The tendency to lean on the arm of flesh instead of trusting in the living God is not Jewish, but human; think not because we read of it in the historical records in the books of the Bible that it is peculiar to the Jews or to the ages or to the dispensations; it is not; but it is an added spiritual peril. The fallacy or misleading notion which it involves is that the Jews were trusting in numbers, looking at the horses and chariots of Egypt -"because they were many" (Isaiah 31)

> *Woe to them that go down to Egypt for help; and stay on horses, and trust in chariots, because they are many; and in horsemen, because they are very strong; but they look not unto the Holy One of Israel, neither seek the LORD!*

We are apt to be imposed upon or obligated by numbers: to think there is safety and even salvation in them, to indulge or ponder the notion that because we are among a great crowd or because we are supported by a very large majority that we are on the side of truth and victory is to invest in false security. Yet, nothing is more misleading; often the vast hosts have been overthrown in conflict by the devoted and determined few; often the small minority, "everywhere spoken against," and despised, has often been proved to be in the right and has ultimately prevailed. If God be on one side and the mightiest multitude on the other, we can be assured of this fact that though the chariots and horses are many, it will be of no account at all with God. Divine providence is not, "by any means necessary" nor victory "on the side of the strongest battalions;" it is the will of God.

How many of us have been devastated or severely hurt because we put our trust in the arms of the flesh. How many times have our hearts been broken because we looked at the size of the ministry thinking that we can develop in what we though was rich and fertile ground. According to Isaiah, Israel apparently trusted in human strength, "in horsemen because they were very strong;" it is a very imposing picture to the eye when we look upon many regiments of cavalrymen and judge on the surface of what we see that they are invincible, overwhelming, and invaluable to us as an ally when the enemy is approaching. They not only appear strong but also well equipped for warfare, but we must consider that we are measuring their worth by how they appear in the time of peace and in the ordinary life of men; yes, the sagacious counselor, the wealthy merchant, the influential statesman or courtier, the mega church, and the renowned evangelist can all do battle and appear to have the strength on which we may build, while the sun is shining, but can they do battle where it counts? At the end of the day, how many hearts have been mended? How many souls have come nigh to Christ? Have they created more weaknesses in ministry than they have healings? We are dazzled with the show of power, the neighing of the war-horse and the glitter of the golden chariot, and the flashing steel of the warriors; they all looked like strength, but God says to Israel, "This is not your strength;" this may succeed for a time, but it is an empire held by the throat, not by the heart."

> Woe to the rebellious children, saith the LORD, that take counsel, but not of me; and that cover with a covering, but not of my Spirit, that they may add sin to sin: 2that walk to go down into Egypt, and have not asked at my mouth; to strengthen themselves in the strength of Pharaoh, and to trust in the shadow of Egypt! 3Therefore shall the strength of Pharaoh be your shame, and the trust in the shadow of Egypt your confusion. 4For his princes were at Zo'an, and his ambassadors came to Hanes. 5They were all ashamed of a people that could not profit them, nor be a help nor profit, but a shame, and also a reproach.

Let us look for a moment at history, when Israel was pure and pious; she was also prosperous. Although Egypt was a far more superior force than Israel, it had no bearing on her deliverance; an undisciplined nation of slaves proved to be too mighty for the cohorts of Pharaoh; in the end it is "righteousness that exalteth a nation," or a church, or an evangelist, or a ministry, "but shame, reproach, and defeat come to those who forsake God."

When we under estimate the elevation God has purposed for us, when we fail to see the power of God in the gifted that He has place in our midst, when we fail to develop the gift of discernment as God has Divinely purposed for us, we will turn to the glitter of apparent success and the strength of numbers for approval, never realizing that "it is not by power, nor by might, but by my spirit."

With gifts come responsibility; with purpose comes duty; we are not only called to be hearers but to be doers as well; if a lake only receives and never gives it becomes stagnant and dangerous; unless the living waters flow through it, it can't sustain any life. If we never step into our purpose or value it as a gift that does not need the strength of numbers, or the approval of the mighty, it will lose its power and we will lose our reward. Purpose demands sacrifice, the giving of ones self; the sun gives up its beams, the ocean exhales its moisture, trees give their fruit, and air passes through the lungs. God has set in order the course of the river and made a pathway for the light of the sun, and they obey His will. Man, unlike nature, can say "No" to God's moral ordination, but not without harm or penalty, but he can, and too often he does; he perverts his gift and turns it into disloyal use, and at other times he neglects it; he "lays up his talent in a napkin."

> And another came, saying, Lord, behold, here is thy pound, which I have kept laid up in a napkin:
>
> Luke 10:20

There is much truth in the saying, "if you don't use it, you lose it." How often do we fail to obey the leading of the Spirit because we don't have confident in our purpose or we believe that someone easy can do what God has called us to do better than we can because their numbers are many and they appear stronger?

Because we tend to trust in the arms of the flesh we neglect to recognize the varied gifts hidden in the soul, gifts of help and healing. We sometimes undervalue our spiritual development; we forget that even the weaker vessel can hold some water; the simplest speech may be eloquent when speaking for the Lord; the slender times with God presents rich opportunities.

> *Neglect not the gift that is in thee, which was given thee by prophecy, with the laying on of the hands of the presbytery.*
>
> *I Timothy 4:14*

We must not neglect our gifts: they will be required of us again.

> *Let no man despise thy youth; but be thou an example of the believers, in word, in conversation, in charity, in spirit, in faith, in purity.*
>
> *I Timothy 4:12*

As pastors of small churches, if we are not mindful of what God has promised, we can create within our congregation atmospheres of doubt and uncertainty. In today's church where success is often measured in numbers or by the popularity of the key speakers we "employ" to preach at our conferences or during fellowship, we can easily hurt our congregations. And I used the term "employ" purposely. Evangelistic Ministry has too often become the convenience of the mega church or the opportunity of the highest bidder; preachers who no longer depend on God to divinely direct them through discernment, now have become "specialist" who preach the same sermon from city to city for the sole purpose of emotionally arousing the people to give of their substance; they preach what they feel the people want to hear (prosperity, blessing without commitment, prophecy that promise hope). As pastors we must not forget that our congregations are our responsibilities and that we must be careful of who we allow to feed them. There is nothing wrong with wanting to have a success fellowship with a popular speaker, but we are warned of God to "try the spirit"; We must believe that God will, if we trust Him, make our visions reality; the success of a fellowship is not in the number that attends nor the popularity of its speaker, but in the fulfillment of it's Divine Purpose; "except the Lord build the house, they that labor, labors but in vain;" if God is not the center of any conference or fellowship, regardless of who the speaker is or how many attend or how successful it appears, the result of it will be failure.

Not trusting in the arms of men is a reoccurring theme throughout the Bible; we see it in the life of Abraham when Sarah decided to allow her handmaid to be the mother who will fulfill the Divine Purpose of God through Abraham's seed; we see it in Isaac when law and tradition said that Esau should be the inheritor of the nation, but God chose Jacob; we see it in Israel when they chose Saul as King, but God divinely chose David. 2 Chronicles 32 give us a true picture of what God can do if we put our trust in Him. He subdued the multitude of King Sennacherib's army and brought shame to the nation simply because Hezekiah consulted God, followed the leading of God, and stood on the promises of God.

> *6Now I know that the LORD saves His anointed; He will answer him from His holy heaven With the saving strength of His right hand. 7Some {boast} in chariots and some in horses, But we will boast in the name of the LORD, our God. 8They have bowed down and fallen, But we have risen and stood upright. 9Save, O LORD; May the King answer us in the day we call.*

David, here realizes that he needs the strength of God to lead the People of God, has request that the people pray for him. Those who know the power of prayer and are not self-exalted must pray for themselves and not despise, but earnestly desire, the prayers of others, even the prayers of those who are subordinate in all respects. Paul often begged of his friends to pray for him. Self-exalted people negate prayer and lean to their own understanding. Those who trust in their own understanding will, with their possessions, be brought down and fail and the possessions they protect will help them in their sinking. Let me leave this thought with you: if you trust in God and not in things or in the arms of man, and obey the scripture you will please God and reap the harvest He has purposed for you.

UNHOLY ATTRACTIONS

One of my favorite pastimes is fishing; as a fisherman I've learned to study the eating habits of certain fish. I noticed that there are certain times when fish can resist the temptation of the bait and at other times they cannot. Fishermen that study the eating habits of fish have also developed "lures" or an artificial bait to further increase the temptation designed to satisfy the fish's appetite. There are other tricks that are use to lure fish to the place where they can be further exposed to temptation. If the fish are able to resist the temptation in the morning, the fishermen will wait until the evening; likewise, the enemy waits for the opportune time to trick the believer into yielding.

You may ask, what does this analogy have to do with "Broken Ribs In Every The Pew", or "Hurt in the congregation." The problem with fish is its appetite; fish have appetites for certain types of "bait" or temptations, and when that appetite is not satisfied by nature the fisherman gains unfair advantage or power over the fish which enables him to hook them. There are believers that have appetites for the unholy or for weighty things of the flesh and for circumstances that hinder their growth in ministry, even though we are admonished to "lay aside these weights and sins." We all know someone who always seem to pick bad fruit: The sister who always chooses men who abuse her, or the believer who is always ending a relationship and starting another; however, temptation does not always involve relationship, some believers can't resist the temptation of shopping while at other times they just neglect major responsibilities; while still others struggle with sexual and other immoralities.

Let me deal with unholy attraction from the perspective of Proverbs 31:30; we find Lemuel's mother warning him against his fascination with superficial charm over genuine beauty (the beauty of the flesh); the process of choosing a wife must first be the attractiveness of the fear of God in a woman over the superficial charm of her worldly countenance. When choosing a companion one must look beyond the temptation of the physical, for in it there is only vanity and temporary admiration; the bloom in the beauty of the face and the grace of form (shape) are only bodily attributes; they have no mental, moral, or spiritual value; they are deceptive; fascination with the physical may cause one to neglect to recognize a more important consideration in choosing a spouse; attributes such as, ill temper, may be taken as strength of character; frivolity or playfulness may be though of as liveliness, and mere softness of disposition could be interpreted as love.

Discovering that you were disillusioned by the physical later on in a relationship may come too late and have no value if your companion turns out not to be the person he or she professed to be. If a relationship does not complement your spiritual development or increase your Christian character, you don't need it. The enemy uses our appetites for what looks good or feels good to trap us as the fisherman used the lure to hook the fish.

Unholy attractions takes place in what I call a "world of make believe". Between time and destiny is purpose; time is the controlling variable; it is controlled by God; we determines our destiny by the choices we make during the time God has allowed us. We live in the reality of a secular world; we respond according to the demands of the flesh; however, we must not forget the words of Paul, *"there is no good thing in the flesh."*

In the secular world of, so called reality, there are other elements: One, *"the world of carnality"*; secondly, *"the world of spirituality"*.

In the temporal world where carnality is the bases of relationship, we tend to lean toward satisfying the flesh; our interest is in the physical and the material and in the pleasing of our fleshly appetites while seeking immediate gratification. The spiritual world is in direct opposition to the world of carnality; its focus is on matters that line up with the Divine Will of God, no matter what the cost; Job declared, *"thou he slay me, yet will I trust him."* One should be concerns with developing the gift of discernment that allows the believer to recognize those who are operating in "the world of make believe;" where we find the source of much of the hidden anxiety that believers experience when they petitioned God for abstract blessings and physical proof that He will answer their request in their favor, or that He will give them the thing they have long waited for.

The Church, the offices we hold, and the principles we live by are sacred; those who serve in or in accord to them must be set apart. There must be an atmosphere of prophetic safety in the Church, those who live according to its principles, trust God for fulfillment of their hopes. The problems that persist in the Church are with the believers who profess and not possess; they operate in the *"world of make believe;"* the believers who trust them (false prophets) and measure the character of other Christians by what they see or feel or hear from them are more likely to be the ones deceived and ultimately hurt by them. As trusting as it may be for a believer to take the word of another saint as truth, the Bible warns us to "try the spirit," because among us are "wolves in sheep clothing." In churches everywhere, in every city there are those who are "real and there are those who are "pretenders;" often it is the "real" who fall victim to the pretender. Too often does the saint find it unnecessary to try other believers to see whether they be of God; trying a person's faith takes time; and too often we are in too big of a hurry to develop a relationship that we miss the vital signs that points to the unholy attributes in a person's character.

Just as there are hurts behind praise and exhalation, there are unholy dispositions behind the smiles, and gratitude of pretenders. Pretenders hide behind acts of good will and expressions of kindness; they use them as the fisherman uses the lure to attract you into their web. In every area of ministry there are pretenders; we are not asked to become "pretender detectives," but we are warn to be aware and that they are present with us, and they look like sheep. You may be attracted to the bee's hive because of the honey, but before you indulge, count up the cost. Pretenders are imitators; the closer they imitate the real thing, the more likely they are to deceive their subject. Pretenders are actor, and the more skillful the actor, the stronger the impression of reality.

We must keep in mind that outward glory becomes a mockery once one's internal wretch is discovered; when ones true character is revealed, his profession or testimony counts for nothing. Keep in mind, when we allow our true worth to be destroyed, the most frantic attempts to recover it at the last moment may prove fruitless; character, once it is lost it is hard to retrieve. It is a common mistake to live for appearance, making the outside of life respectable while the heart is corrupt. Some people are more anxious to seem good than to be good. What use is purple and fine linen to the leper?

Just because we have asked God for gifts, and the prophet has prophesied that the gifts are coming does not mean that we should accept the first image of those gifts as the real thing; Satan is in the manufacturing business, and he can produce counterfeits of any gifts we ask of God. Satan knows that most believers look at the physical, so he deceives us through the members of our flesh, and creates a counterfeit of what we asked for and what the prophet said was coming; if we are not careful to discern what spirit the gift that has come to us have, we will be drawn by unholy attraction into a relationship, or into some circumstance, or situation that will lead to the destruction of our Christian character.

What we entertain in a moment of weakness can become an adverse action we regret for a lifetime; it is better to lose ones coat than ones virtue (Joseph), it is better to lose ones position than to lose ones integrity, and to lose one freedom than to lose ones favor with God.

James, in his epistle, drew for us a powerful picture of the results of those who entertain lustful thoughts (James 1:13-15). Lust is like a raging fire that has the power to devour a person. We cannot stop lustful thoughts from coming to us, but we can refuse to entertain and/or dwell on them. Thoughts work like magnets that pulls an attracts objects toward them. When inner desires connect with outer circumstances, there is an enticement to take a bite of the forbidden fruit. It is always dangerous to allow ourselves the titillation of thinking about forbidden fruit; eventually, we will encounter the fruit and there will be no barrier (physical or mental) to prevent us from indulging. Temptations may cause us to stumble, but we determine whether we fall.

Church Alive, World Aflame Pub. Page 34 summer

The accessibility of a thing increases its power of temptation; we cannot be tempted by a thing to which we have no accessibility. Potiphar's wife was attracted to Joseph because he was accessible to her. There are many things in this world that are wonderfully and beautifully made, but they do not tempt us; they cannot because they are not accessible to us.

We must discover how to determine when promised expectations are not unholy attraction or temptations. Questioning what appears to be prophetic fulfillment is the key. No matter what it looks like or sounds like or feels like, try it by the spirit (the Word).

I called those who deceive the flock pretenders, but the Bible refers to them as hypocrites, as wolves in sheep clothing going among the flock like raving wolves; this is not a New Testament phenomenon; we see the infiltration of the enemy in Ezekiel; the Lord refers to prophets in the midst of the congregation like roaring lion and ravening wolves devouring the souls of the people.

[Verse 27 in Original Hebrew]

23 And the word of the LORD came unto me, saying, 24 Son of man, say unto her, Thou art the land that is not cleansed, nor rained upon in the day of indignation. 25 There is a conspiracy of her prophets in the midst thereof, like a roaring lion ravening the prey; they have devoured souls; they have taken the treasure and precious things; they have made her many widows in the midst thereof. 26 Her priests have violated [F95] my law, and have profaned mine holy things: they have put no difference between the holy and profane, neither have they shewed difference between the unclean and the clean, and have hid their eyes from my sabbaths, and I am profaned among them. 27 Her princes in the midst thereof are like wolves ravening the prey, to shed blood, and to destroy souls, to get dishonest gain. 28 And her prophets have daubed them with untempered morter, seeing vanity, and divining lies unto them, saying, Thus saith the Lord GOD, when the LORD hath not spoken. 29 The people of the land have used oppression, [F96] and exercised robbery, and have vexed the poor and needy: yea, they have oppressed the stranger wrongfully. 30 And I sought for a man among them, that should make up the hedge, and stand in the gap before me for the land, that I should not destroy it: but I found none. 31 Therefore have I poured out mine indignation upon them; I have consumed them with the fire of my wrath: their own way have I recompensed upon their heads, saith the Lord GOD.

Ezekiel 22:23-31

The enemy has always sought to destroy the Church from within and without; he waits like a war horse for the opportune moment to attack; Habakkuk liken him to a creature of the night that preys upon the weaker and less subtle, the eagle, the leopard, the galloping horseman. Matthews, Luke, and Acts simply calls them wolves in sheep clothing, hypocrites. How many times have we witnessed in our own congregations saints befriending each other, the hypocrite and the poor innocent sheep who becomes the victims of deception by the very ones they should be trusting in ministry. From the pulpit to the door the spirit of deception waits for the opportunity to lure an innocent soul into its web.

The intent to deceive constitutes the essence of lying. Truth is the representation of things as they are; however, truth may be departed from in many ways without the intent to deceive, but veracity or should I say, truthfulness, is always obligatory. Some say that there are times when intentional deceit is justified, but according to St. Augustine, "whoso thinketh that there is any kind of lie which is not sin, deceiveth himself.

Deceit takes many forms; it may be direct equivocation, suppression of truth, frauds, or malicious; deceit marked by hatred and malice are the worst and most reprehensive. David in chapter 21 in the book of I Samuel sets out to deceive the priest, Ahimelech, by telling his that he was on a secret mission for the king; what we do not see in this deceit is hatred or malice, but the question is, was there Justification?

When David present himself alone before the high priest he was pressed with hunger and fear; therefore, he is tempted to invent a falsehood, but need does not constitute justification for deception. If David had trusted God his need would have probably been met. David thought that no harm could come from this deceit; but when we decide to deceive we do not know to what end it will bring us. "Oh what a tingled web we weave when we seek to deceive." How many times have we witnessed little "no-harm", so called "white lies" turn into the center of conflict? We often hear the phrase "I lied to you because I love you." "White lies" hurt worst when the reality of the truth is realized and the affects of it has entangled a greater host of individuals. We are often the victims of unholy attractions because we fail to weigh the circumstances of our current realities. That is to say, we tend to make commitments in relationship before we are sure that it is a relationship we should be in. Most all unholy attractions turn out to be parasitic, the stronger individual feeding off of the weaker or should I say the person with the low self-esteem becomes the victim in the relationship.

Let me end the chapter with a story told to me by a friend, Sanni; she came to America from Nigeria; her family was very religious, and her father very stern; she was the middle child with two older sisters and a younger sister and brother. Her father was a teacher and laid a good foundation for his children to develop a hunger for education and excellence. Sanni understood the cost of sending four children to school at the same time so she made a decision to go live with an aunt who promised to incur the cost of her schooling. Sanni's parents did not want her to accept this offer, but would not sway Sanni's trust in her aunt by marring her aunt's character. It was Sanni's responsibility to count up the cost, to weigh the circumstances by trying the spirit by the teaching she had received. Like so many in ministry, Sanni looked on the physical and maid her decision by what she saw in the status of her aunt (the business of imports and exports, the superfluous nature of her character, and what seemed to be the ability of her aunt to pay the cost of her schooling). Again, we are deceived by promises and unholy attracted to the physical. Needless to say, Sanni went to live with her aunt, and was used and treated like a servant, (she was forced to do the cleaning, cooking, washing....and other household chores while at the same time, go to school), only to discover at the end of the semester that her aunt had no intention of paying the cost of her schooling. Returning to her father's house she discovered that her attraction to the physical affected the lives of others in her circle. Remember this, "Lean not to your own understanding, but in all thou way acknowledge God and He will direct your path."

CONDITIONED

I n my many years of working in the adult learning field, mostly with under privileged and disadvantaged student, I discovered that many of those who suffer in poverty do so because they have been unconsciously conditioned to suffer. I wondered why a large number of students could never get to school on time, and when they got there why they were not motivated to work hard academically, but found pleasure in putting all of their energy in finding ways to evade doing any school work, and in some instances they took issues with students who preferred to get good grades. The key phrase here is "unconsciously conditioned;" in ministry we might refer to this as a generational curse (a condition that is passed down from one generation to the next). In other words, a child might do something a certain way because his or her father or mother did it that way; they may dislike a person or a thing because their mother disliked it. It is the job of ministry to un-condition the conditioned.

The un-conditioning of conditions is a tedious ministry; we must be careful not to further exacerbate the condition. We must keep in mind that this conditioning is hidden in the neuron portion of the brain; the individual, in all practicality, feels that he or she is right in his or her thinking. Remember, "truth" is what we believe it to be"; this does not mean what we believe is true; therefore, we must minister to the mind; "thinking make it so…..; our focus must be on getting the individual to think differently.

6 Eat thou not the bread of him that hath an evil eye, neither desire thou his dainty meats: 7 For as he thinketh in his heart, so is he: Eat and drink, saith he to thee; but his heart is not with thee. 8 The morsel which thou hast eaten shalt thou vomit up, and lose thy sweet words. Proverbs 23:6-8

Paul speaks to us in Romans 12 and reminds us that we are not to conform to the standards or circumstances in our environment; we must not accept them as, "that's the way it has to be", but be ye therefore changed by your thinking.

And be not conformed to this world: but be ye transformed by the renewing of your mind, that ye may prove what is that good, and acceptable, and perfect, will of God.

Romans12:2

When ministering to believers who have been unconsciously conditioned to a specific mind set, we must be careful not to create an atmosphere that threatens their self-esteem; when ones self-esteem is threatened an environment of anxiety is created.

And, ye fathers, provoke not your children to wrath: but bring them up in the nurture and admonition of the Lord.

Ephesians 6:4

In an experiment using shuttle boxes and dogs, an atmosphere of helplessness was created; dogs were place in shuttle boxes that were designed with two compartments: one for resting and the other for feeding; during the first phase of the experiment one group of dogs experienced the dimming of a light just before feeding; the dogs soon learned that dimming the light meant feeding. The second phase of the experiment involved the dogs getting a shock just after the light started to dim; the dogs soon learned in order to avoid the shock, they had to jump out of that portion of the box at the moment the light started to dim. To create an environment of hopelessness, the dogs had to be prevented from escaping the shock. This occurred during the third phase of the experiment; the dogs were placed into harnesses so that when the light was dimed and the floor of the cage electrified, the dogs could not evade the shock. The dogs soon learned that they could not escape the evitable shock; therefore they gave up and resigned to a hopeless disposition. Once it was determined that the dogs had resigned to this hopelessness, they were removed from the electrified cages to a safe and secured environment, but although the dogs were out of danger of being shocked they still resigned to there hopeless disposition.

In ministry there are believers who are living in hopeless situations or under hopeless conditions; finding Grace and security through the Gospel of Jesus Christ has put them in the ark of safety and out of the enemy's camp, and off of the electrified floor, but like the dogs they still resigned to their hopelessness, and although they are free by the blood of Jesus, they are living beneath their privilege and some even die, never really tasting the Grace of God. The question then is how do we turn the hopelessness of a believer into hope in Christ Jesus? The dogs had to be dragged from the place where the seed of hopelessness was planted and forced to experience safety and security in a new place. In ministry we must expose the hopeless to divinely inspired preaching of the word of God and true worship. "Faith comes by hearing". The dogs needed physical intervention to bring them to a place of safety, but in ministry there is no moral, spiritual or mental value in the physical. Change in Christian character comes by "faith" and faith comes by hearing, and hearing by the Word of God. We must change the way the hopeless think; "Let this mind be in you that is in Christ Jesus." I began this chapter by referring to students who had never seen anyone in their household get up in the morning to go to work. There are believers who have never been exposed to true worship; they have never felt the anointing power of God; their only exposure to the real power of God has been through a "form of godliness;" a counterfeit of God's powerful anointing.

The hopeless must be ministered to by true believers; preferable by one who has himself experienced the power of God's deliverance; someone who, without a shadow of doubt, believes that God can. Keep in mind that "faith comes by hearing;" we must encourage the hopeless to hear sound ministering and protect them from those ministries that will drive them further into their hopelessness. "Beware of false prophets, gainsayers, busybodies;" we all know those within our ministries who are the nucleus or the seedbed of controversy in our congregations; they are the ones that are always in the middle of every unpleasant situation; they themselves have need of deliverance.

As easy as it may seem, ministering to the spiritually blind or unconsciously conditioned or the hopeless is a ministry that requires sacrifice, commitment, dedication, and devotion. The urge to give up is ever present in the mind of the believer; the enemy constantly seeks to discourage us and derail our efforts, but for every word of discouragement uttered by the enemy, we can hear the voice of God crying out through the scriptures, "Stand!, after you have done all, stand anyhow." In Paul's letter to the Ephesians he admonishes them: first, before trying to deliver any one else, put on the whole armor of God, "be strong." This is not an exercise of fleshly warfare; it is one of spiritual weakness.

> *[10]Finally, my brethren, be strong in the Lord, and in the power of his might. [11]Put on the whole armour of God, that ye may be able to stand against the wiles of the devil. [12]For we wrestle not against flesh and blood, but against principalities, against powers, against the rulers of the darkness of this world, against spiritual wickedness in high places. [13]Wherefore take unto you*

the whole armour of God, that ye may be able to withstand in the evil day, and having done all, to stand. [14]Stand therefore, having your loins girt about with truth, and having on the breastplate of righteousness; [15]And your feet shod with the preparation of the gospel of peace; [16]Above all, taking the shield of faith, wherewith ye shall be able to quench all the fiery darts of the wicked. [17]And take the helmet of salvation, and the sword of the Spirit, which is the word of God: [18]Praying always with all prayer and supplication in the Spirit, and watching thereunto with all perseverance and supplication for all saints; [19]And for me, that utterance may be given unto me, that I may open my mouth boldly, to make known the mystery of the gospel,

Eph 6:10-19

Hopelessness that has developed from a seedbed of spiritual weakness is deeply rooted in the mindset of the hopeless; those who may have never been exposed to the reality of the truth, may have, for all of their Christian lives, been influenced by the rudiments of the flesh in which they moved and have had their being. Coming into the knowledge of God and abiding under the Graces of God does not mean that one bears the fruit of Godliness. Great fruit vines take time to bear good fruit. We are born out of hopelessness into the liberty of Grafted, and like the Gentiles, we were not included in the Law of Moses (Rom 2:14), but were grafted into a good olive tree and called the people of God, contrary to nature.

The process of bring deliverance from hopelessness begins with first putting on the whole armor of God; as they say on the air plane "put on your life jacket first" then help someone else; the blind cannot lead the blind neither can the hopeless bring deliverance to the hopeless.

The state education system in its evaluation of students, label some as "special ed."; this puts them into a special group; the label "special ed."

54

carries with it the stigma that these people should be treated differently because they are troublesome and hard to get along with. Many of these individuals are hopelessly moved through the "system" never being treated for their problem; only the symptoms of their problems of treated. In ministry we must deal with the root of hopelessness. Just as we help sinners rid themselves of the penalty of sin, we must help the hopeless rid themselves from their hopelessness. Hopelessness is like a plant that produces fruit of its kind; hopelessness can only produce more hopelessness.

If we see sin as the mother of hopelessness; we can then understand that the potential to revert to a hopeless condition will always be with us because there is no good thing in the flesh. Therefore, if the potential of hopelessness still remain, we must limit or control the fruit it bears. Paul concluded that the seed of sin is ever with me, when I want to do good I cannot because the root of sin remains in my flesh; the thing I do not want to do, I do; likewise is the frustration of the hopeless. We must treat the seedbed of hopelessness (the flesh) with an insecticide (the word of God, prayer and fasting) that will kill and limit the production of its symptoms or its affect of hopelessness.

There are times in ministry when our own situations seem hopeless and we ourselves are casted into hopelessness. As we reflect on the life of Jonah and how hopeless his situation must have seemed, we cannot but see ourselves.

> *15 So they took up Jonah, and cast him forth into the sea: and the sea ceased from her raging. 16 Then the men feared the LORD exceedingly, and offered a sacrifice unto the LORD, and made vows. 17 Now the LORD had prepared a great fish to swallow up Jonah. And Jonah was in the belly of the fish three days and three nights. Jonah 2:1 Then Jonah prayed unto the LORD his God out of the fish's belly, Jonah 1:15-2:1*

Perhaps Jonah was just tired and wanted to have some private time for himself; perhaps during the next week he would have found time to go to Nineveh and preach the Word of God. How many times have we put off doing what God has told us to do? Procrastination is one of the gateways to developing a hopeless situation; it fosters negative thought and pessimism. Putting off doing what God has told us to do leads to a lose of interest in doing it at all; this is another trick of the enemy; I'm reminded of a story about three devils trying to impress Satan. The first devil tells Satan that he'll tempt mankind to commit all sorts of sexual sins….The second tells him that he'll tempt mankind to commit all sorts of abuses, but the third one was more shrewd, "I'll tell them to do all the good works they can…but I'll tell them to do it tomorrow…" Satan uses procrastination or "wait" to keep us right where we are. If we wait we will never rid ourselves of any hopeless situation.

> *We know what we should do, but we do not do it.*
> *We know we should have gotten the oil changed …*
> *We know we should have stopped for gas…*
> *We know we should have bought that snow shovel…*
> *We know we should have studied for that exam…*
> *We know we should have checked on the kids…*
> *We know we should have saved up some money for the taxes…*
> *We know what we should have done, but we didn't do it.*
> *http://jonathanjordan.squarespace.com/sermon-notes/2007/9/14/*
> *antidote-for-hopelessness-its-never-too-late-to-pray.html*

In our effort to escape doing what God has told us to do, we often find ourselves in a worse situation. The omniscience and omnipresence of God makes it impossible for us to escape God's command; regardless of what we do that is right, we will never be delivered out of hopelessness unless or until we do the one thing that God has told us to do. Whether we created our own hopeless state or whether it is the product of a generational curse, it is a stage for God's miraculous power to be manifested.

Look at the situation you find yourself in; compare it to that of Jonah: He ran from the presence of God, he refuse to obey God, he was found by God and confessed his fault and submit to the will of God; he was thrown overboard and swallowed by a fish. From looking at your situation, as it was with Jonah, things must have looked pretty hopeless; as Jonah choked on seaweed and was terrified by the great fish, you too, must be horrified by the pressure of your hopelessness. There are times when we feel that our prayers are not being heard and that our situation is a punishment from God. Although God sometimes use the pressures of life and the situations we put ourselves in, to force us to go in a direction that we should have chosen for ourselves, we should not think of our situation as being too bad, nor should we feel that we have angered God too often; we should not think of it as a punishment or think for a moment that our prayers will not be heard. How was Jonah able to rid himself of the hopelessness in his situation? What did he do to get God's attention? Let us evaluate, firstly, as we previously stated, he resigned to the Will of God; secondly, he confessed his error and accepted fate as God had predestined it; thirdly, he remember what God had command. When we get into trouble, we must remember what God has said in His promises, "look toward the holy temple".

> Then Jonah prayed unto the LORD his God out of the fish's belly, ²and said, I cried by reason of mine affliction unto the LORD, and he heard me; out of the belly of hell cried I, and thou heardest my voice. Then I said, I am cast out of thy sight; yet I will look again toward thy holy temple.

I cried by reason of mine hopelessness: My drug addiction, my alcoholism, my sexual deviance, by reason of my poverty, bankruptcy, joblessness, pending divorce, failing health, lack of education (school drop out), the loss of my children, pending imprisonment.

If we go by what we see or hear or feel, our situations will always seem hopeless; we must keep in mind that regardless of what it looks like, there is hope through Christ Jesus. Prayer, fasting, commitment, dedication and devotion turn vision into reality. To change a hopeless situation into hope, the hopeless must see themselves functioning outside of or above their hopeless situation.

For Jonah it must have been an easy task to gather enough faith to trust God in the time of crisis, after all, he was a preacher; but for many, hopelessness has been a lifelong conditioning, and when you've not been exposed to liberty, you don't know what freedom really is, or what the reality of prayer is; especially when you think you are already free. As a young boy growing up in Pompano during the 50's and 60's, I didn't know I was poor; it wasn't until someone told me that I was poor that I knew it. There were certain foods I never had eaten until I left Pompano; there were also other foods I preferred than some, outside of my community, would not think of eating. In ministry there are certain liberties that some have never experienced, and are relatively pleased with living beneath their privilege (unconsciously).

> *And another dieth in the bitterness of his soul, and never eateth with pleasure. Job 21:25 King James Version*

> *While another dies with a bitter soul, never even tasting {anything} good. Job 21:25 New American Standard Version*

Some will never come to reality of the truth; they will never submit to the reality of their conditioning; they will see your effort to cure their hopelessness as an attempt to belittle their righteousness. They will continue to go to church, Bible class, Sunday school, conferences, seminars, *"ever learning but never able to come to the knowledge or the truth"*

2 Timothy 3:7

In the world of skepticism it is said there are those who know and know not that they know, enlighten them; there are those who know not and know that they know not, teach them; there is a group that know not and think that they know, shun them. In ministry we must seek to bring all men to the reality of the truth; whether it is in the knowledge of God's Word or the knowledge of ones character.

"It is not God's will that any should perish, but that all should come to repentance."

1 Peter 3:7

It is not uncommon in ministry to find believers who are not aware of their spiritual disposition. They feel that spiritual unction gives them the right to say or act out what they feel; giving no thought of the feelings others. The hopeless may be wrong in their thinking, and may wound others by their unholy disposition, but the body of Christ, baptized believers who are steadfast and unmovable must be willing and ready to sacrifice time and effort to bring them (the hopeless) unto the reality of the truth with out further wounding them. We must keep in mind that words out of the mouth of careless believers are instruments in the hands of the enemy. Words can kill and destroy in a moment's time what it took a lifetime to build.

The power of life and death are in the tongue.

Proverbs 18:21

Even so the tongue is a little member, and boasteth great things. Behold, how great a matter a little fire kindleth!

James 3:5

And the tongue is a fire, a world of iniquity: so is the tongue among our members, that it defileth the whole body, and setteth on fire the course of nature; and it is set on fire of hell.

<u>*Jas 3:6*</u>

But the tongue can no man tame; it is an unruly evil, full of deadly poison.

James 3:8

Without dough, the strongest weapon we have against hopeless is faith, and faith comes by hearing. What we say and how we say it is important as we work to win others for the cause of Christ. Having the Gospel and not being able to deliver it in a manner that will draw men to Christ is paramount to not have it at all.

A NOW CIRCUMSTANCE

S atan has held men and women in the body of Christ hostage to their own conditionings far too long; far too long have they lived beneath their privilege without ever stepping into their promised purpose. Weaknesses in Man's faith have been the real reason that underlay his failures. Faith causes us to move positively toward the things we think about; faith is what makes the abstract reality and the intangible tangible; it is the substance of things hoped for; the evidence of thing not seen.

The lack of faith is the seedbed of procrastination, the source of our willingness to accept what is…. For what can be. We have been promised the desires of our hearts and the benefit of whatever we ask for in the name of Jesus, but Satan has blinded our eyes and deafened our ears so that we cannot put into action what we believe. There is an urgent need for the immediate transformation of our faith; we must move from just carnal faith, to "Now Faith;" carnal faith is based on what can be obtained through temporal means, through what the members of our flesh esteem worthy of a greater state. Carnal faith says we need money or some tangible substance or education or friendship, and most of all "time" to be what we desire or to obtain the things we want.

"Now Faith" says we only need a relationship with God and the courage to believe that He is a rewarder to them that diligently seek Him, (Hebrews 1:6) "Now Faith" says "it is," the minute we believe it is. The secret to "Now Faith" is knowledge; "faith comes by hearing;" the more we learn about what God can do and why, the more likely we will trust him and increase our faith in Him. If a man lacks knowledge (wisdom) let him ask God. All knowledge is not pure, (Malachi 2:7) "For the priest shall keep pure the knowledge," "wisdom is the principle thing, therefore get wisdom, and with all thou getting, get understanding, (James 1:6). As much as we are admonished to believe that faith come by hearing, we are not to believe every thing we hear, nor every spirit we encounter, but we are admonished as fore stated in previous chapters, to "try the spirit" for there are among us, false prophets, wolves in sheep clothing; "Now Faith" cannot be developed from misinterpreted knowledge; "in all thou getting, get understanding." Some men hear God and understand what He means, such as Abel; other men hear God and miss the real meaning of what he wants, such as Cain.

"Now Faith" says I'm healed when the doctor's diagnoses is fatal; "Now Faith" says you're free when the evidence points to your guilt. "Now Faith" supplies the outcome when your circumstances say there is no other way out or you can't afford it. Time is running out for us to increase our faith; when God speaks, its for our immediate action; obedience is far greater in the sight of God than any sacrifice can ever be. You will never get out of sacrifice what you can get out of obedience.

"Now Faith" refutes the past and points to the present; it infers a change of course, a change of principles, "old things are passed away" and a new day is begun, a new season, new opportunities to step into ones purpose. There are noticeable "Now Situations" in the scripture; Genesis 12:19, A "now" situation that changed the disposition of Abraham and the direction in which he was headed, physically and psychologically. There comes a time in all of our lives when we will be faced with a "Now Circumstance;" a time when we will have to act according to God's divine purpose. For Abraham it was time for God's Divine Plan of Salvation to enter a stage in which Abraham was a "key" player. The

"Now Situation" in verse19 changed Abraham's thinking; we are not made perfect in our first encounter with God, but the process begins when we hear and obey the Lord when He says to us, "Now."

Let us revisit our definition of "Now:" we first established that "Now" is at the present time or "is" the present. Because Jesus has already paid the cost of our salvation and the price of our deliverance, we are healed of our hurts and delivered from our conditions, "Now"; all we need to do is claim them. Suffer we must, for it is the badge of the faithful; "if we suffer with Him we will reign with Him." It is our suffering that shapes our disposition and forms our attitude toward others. The time of our call to purpose is divinely appointed; at that set time the choice is ours; we then may chose to continue in our suffering and endurance or we may submit to the predestined will of God.

Zacchaeus in Luke 19 was faced with his 'Now Circumstance," verse 5 "Make hast and come down," it was at that moment that Zaccheaus had the power to determine his purpose; verse 8, "Behold, Lord, the half of my goods I give to the poor; and if I have taken anything from any man by false accusation, I restore him fourfold" "The power of life and death is in the tongue," Proverbs 18:21. Confession, repentance, and admittance are the first steps in deliverance from the hurts we have suffered with for so long. "Now Faith" lets us see ourselves above our situations and beyond our circumstances; with it we "call those things that are not as if they were;"

> If there by any consolation in Christ, if any comfort of love, if any fellowship of the spirit if any bowels and mercies, ² Fulfil ye my joy, that ye be likeminded, having the same love, being of one accord, of one mind. ³ Let nothing be done through strife or vainglory; but in lowliness of mind let each esteem other better than themselves. ⁴ Look not every man on his own things, but every man also on the things of others. ⁵ Let this mind be in you,

which was also in Christ Jesus: [6] Who, being in the form of God, thought it not robbery to be equal with God: [7] But made himself of no reputation, and took upon him the form of a servant, and was made in the likeness of men: [8] And being found in fashion as a man, he humbled himself, and became obedient unto death, even the death of the cross. [9] Wherefore God also hath highly exalted him, and given him a name which is above every name: [10] That at the name of Jesus every knee should bow, of things in heaven, and things in earth, and things under the earth; [11] And that every tongue should confess that Jesus Christ is Lord, to the glory of God the Father

The tone of these verses personifies the change in Zacchaeus' character; that which was hidden of him is now open before all. Openness serves the victims of hurt well; it is a form of repentance; admitting that there is a problem is usually the first sign of deliverance, bring oneself face to face with his "Now Circumstance."

Often we delay our deliverance because of our dependence on other; The man that lay at the pool said, "I have no one to put me in the pool: for 38 years the man depended on someone else for his healing; he had not yet come face to face with his "Now Circumstance;" it wasn't until Jesus gave him the choice that he found Grace in the sight of God to do something about his circumstance. "No man can come to me, except the Father which has sent me draw him: and I will raise him up at the last day" (John 6:44).

We must be visual and watchful in our course; we must trust God in all our ways, leaning not to our own understanding. Throughout life we will be faced with opportunities for change, opportunities to step into purpose; to be healed or delivered or freed from some condition; we must never allow Satan to blind our eyes to the mystery of Godliness or deafen our ears from the voice of God; for faith comes by hearing, and if we miss God's message we are doomed to suffer the consequences.

THE LONG WAY AROUND
FOR A BETTER VIEW

L et's start this chapter by quoting Elder Corey Oshikoya and Bishop Shelvis Green whose sermons became the subject of this chapter. Elder Oshikoya used Israel's history as founded in Exodus, chapters 15, 16, and 13 to draw a conclusion that God sometimes takes us the long way around to bring us to our divine purpose. Bishop Green concluded from Mark's writings of the blind man; some believers fail to step into purpose because they have been blinded to what God has divinely purposed for them.

As we revisit Exodus 15:22-26, we discover that God's care for Israel was beyond her comprehension of His purpose for her. Here we learn that Israel equated freedom with the pleasures of life; to satisfy them He gave them sweet waters. At some point in our lives we will come to a place called Marah (bitterness) before we can clearly see where God is trying to take us. The Omnipotent God can give us our heart's desire without allowing us to ever experiencing hurt or trial, but God's interest in us starts with the development of our Christian Character. Elder Oshikoya puts it this way, God isn't interested in us reaching a destiny as we have planned it for ourselves, but rather He is interested in the development of our character according to His divine purpose. God wants to move us to a different level or according to Dr. Aretha Wilson's revelation, to a new dimension. Destiny infers completion, the end of the journey, but dimension infers the continued enlarging of our territorial growth and development in Christ Jesus.

> *So Moses brought Israel from the Red sea, and they went out into the wilderness of Shur; and they went three days in the wilderness, and found no water. ²³ And when they came to Marah, they could not drink of the waters of Marah, for they were bitter: therefore the name of it was called Marah. ²⁴ And the people murmured against Moses, saying, What shall we drink? ²⁵ And he cried unto the LORD; and the LORD shewed him a tree, which when he had cast into the waters, the waters were made sweet: there he made for them a statute and an ordinance, and there he proved them, ²⁶ And said, If thou wilt diligently hearken to the voice of the LORD thy God, and wilt do that which is right in his sight, and wilt give ear to his commandments, and keep all his statutes, I will put none of these diseases upon thee, which I have brought upon the Egyptians: for I am the LORD that healeth thee.*
>
> *Exodus 15:22*

A new dimension in Christ does not come without scarify. God knows that some of us are babes and that exposure to certain kind of conflict may discourage us as we walk toward grace, therefore He has designed our development as believers to be a process: milk, bread, meat, and so on (Exodus 13:17-18).

> *And it came to pass, when Pharaoh had let the people go, that God led them not through the way of the land of the Philistines, although that was near; for God said, Lest peradventure the people repent when they see war, and they return to Egypt: ¹⁸ But God led the people about, through the way of the wilderness of the Red sea: and the children of Israel went up harnessed [F43] out of the land of Egypt.*

God knew that just seeing the war, the conflict, and the sorrows of others would have driven Israel back into slavery; He knew that because of her slavery she had become institutionalized. A study of the criminal justice system shows that in a California prison system, 85 percent of women in the jail have been there before; in New York City 65 percent of the prisoners are repeat offenders. The institutionalization of a prisoner occurs when a prisoner no longer believers that he or she can function on their in a free society; this belief develops unknowingly to the prisoner; revisit the chapter on unconscious conditioning.

Israel, like so many who suffer in ministry, had become institutionalized. They said to Moses, we would rather be slaves in Egypt with bread to eat than to be free in the wilderness hungry. Satan wants you to believe that you would rather be battered in a house than free in a shelter; he wants to believe that you will be happier living the life of a prostitute driving a BMW than you will be free taking the bus. Satan would have you buy groceries with stolen money than to be free while standing on food pantry line. When we feel safer in bondage than we do free having to make sacrifices, we have become institutionalized or condition to a sin driven life. Institutionalization causes spiritual blindness.

God, knew what seeing the conflict of other nations would do to Israel's faith, took her the long way around. You may ask, why must the righteous suffer the long way around? First, it fosters the tries of our faith; "God's ways are not our ways" as fore stated, God wants to first develop our character, not our gifts or our relationship; gifts deceive us as to our true value in ministry and in a relationships; who we are connected to determines where we go with our vision; therefore when our gifts fail or our relationships cease we no longer have the source to turn our visions into reality, but with a good Christian character you are connect to God the source of all things present and things to come.

God took Israel the long way around so that she could get a better view of herself. Too many believers can't see themselves because they are looking at themselves from within, but, if you are a sinner who: walk like a sinner, talk like a sinner, act like a sinner, dress like a sinner, then being a sinner looks pretty good from your perspective. God doesn't see us the way we are, He sees us for what we can be. We need only to look in the scripture and see that all who God called saw themselves not worthy of their calling. If you have fail to respond to God's call because you measured your spiritual worth by what you know about yourself, you are living beneath your privilege; although Abraham was a heathen, a liar, and doubtful God saw him as the father of faith; although Gideon was afraid and hiding under the wine press, God saw him as a man of valor; although David was an adulterer and a murderer God saw him as the apple of His eye. If we allow God to direct our paths, we will end up just where we aught to be; our purpose will be realized and God's promises to us fulfilled.

ENVY

A nother fruit that falls from the tree of jealousy is envy; it too stems from resentment. To understand how it affects our Christian maturity and spiritual development, we will look at the third chapter of Esther. Haman's resentment of the Jews led to an unexplainable hatred for Mordecai, the king's cup bearer.

Before we deal with Haman's envy, let's look at his character and his disposition. Haman was promoted above all the princes serving in his region; they were commanded to give reverence to him which is another way of saying worship him. The king was infatuated with Haman and seemed unable to refuse him any request. Haman's sudden success was a surprise to everyone, but not with out price; you must keep in mind that "sudden or easy success is not a benefit," however, it is noteworthy to know that in most of us there is a hidden carving for success.

My mother use to say to me "nothing is worth have if you don't have to work for it;" we enjoy prosperity better when it is the result of our own hard labor; it is a sweeter and more honorable possession when it comes as the reward for a conscious effort; we must infer that Haman's rise to power was not the result of any admirable personal qualities or for any important services he rendered. What the record shows that there was an atmosphere of suspicion around his elevation that was degrading to both himself and the king; we must be mindful that those who are suddenly elevated to abnormal levels of success tend not to follow the rule of legitimate achievement.

The Lord's eyes are upon us all the time; Haman would not be allowed to enjoy his ill-gotten position without trouble. From the outset he became annoyed with Mordecai; this led to tragic results. If we contrast between those who love God and those who love the praise of men, we would find that those who love God are the real victors. Mordecai stumbled upon a plot to kill the king; to prevent the assassination he sat at the door of the king's chamber not allowing this assassination to take place. When it was discovered what Mordecai had done, it was written in the book of record. Believing that the assassination was ordered by Haman, Mordecai refuse to reverence him, but rather stood erect with no fear when he was in Haman's presence. It must have been a sight to see, a man, too noble to bend to the world's perception of honor while all others stooped in slavish adulation. As the Holy Sprit separates the believer from the unbeliever, Mordecai's boldness created a gulf between himself and his companions. There comes a time when we must stand, even if we have to stand alone. Again, "I would rather be right alone than to be wrong with a thousand," this is a quote from a popular radio program. Individual boldness often attracts the attention of others; Mordecai's companions notices his disharmony and admonished him to give in to the press of Haman, but "he hearkened not unto them." Every one who comes to you, questioning your actions does not have your interest at heart. Sincere inquiry is to be encouraged and kindly welcomed; it is the interfering curiosity into the affairs of others that is to be rejected. Paul and Peter called them "Busy-bodies."

> *For we hear that there are some which walk among you disorderly, working not at all, but are busy-bodies.*
>
> *Now them that are such we command and exhort by our Lord Jesus Christ, that with quietness they work, and eat their own bread. But ye, brethren, be not weary in well doing.*
>
> *2 Thessalonians 3:11-13*

But let none of you suffer as a murderer, or as a thief, or as an evildoer, or as a busy-body in other men's matters. Yet if any man suffer as a Christian, let him not be ashamed; but let him glorify God on this behalf.

Peter 4:15-16 1

Mordecai, overcome by the harassment of his companions, or their perception that his continued silence was an indication of him being afraid to speak out, emphatically declared that he too was a Jew and that that was the reason why he could not abase himself, as they did, before Haman.

What was meant to satisfy their concern infuriated them even more; they took his reason to mean that he though himself to be superior to them. They were hurt, their pride was wounded, this awakened a more evil curiosity; it was mean and wicked of them, but they told Haman that Mordecai was really a Jew, and expected that because Haman was the all powerful favorite of the king that he would compel Mordecai to behave more harmoniously with them. Believer that bend to the winds of the enemy or worldly fashion often conceive malice toward those who are stronger than they are in principle or self-respect.

The sight of Mordecai standing upright among the prostrate attendants of the palace filled Haman with a fierce and vindictive wrath. True greatness is above bigheartedness; it is above resenting little offenses; true greatness does not rest on the humiliation of others. Haman's glory was tarnished, and his happiness marked by the stubbornness of one man who occupied a lower position compared to his own. Mordecai was just a fly in the ointment of his pride. We should not allow the disposition of others to affect the divine appointment or purpose for which we have been called. There will always be those who do not understand your purpose or who will do their best to prescribe for you what they feel God has given you to do. Doubt and fear always spring up in those who occupy ill-gotten positions; they imagine offense or insult when none is intended; they magnify small annoyances into hostile attacks on their character. Those who rise to unworthy levels of favor have within them the seed of punishment; their biggest enemy is themselves.

Envy does not measure the evil it contemplates; it is like the tide that overflows it boundaries and washes away the soil that nourishes the fruit tree from which it eats. It throws away the shield and only swings the sword blindly; every feeling of pity is quenched in its fire; its only aim is to cause what suffering it can. When the fires of envy begin to burn, it easily finds fuel to feed it. Those who are possessed by it are blind to the considerations that should modify or temper it; they become sharp sighted in regards or respect to thing that will stimulate their anger.

It was bad enough for Mordecai to not reverence Haman, but when Haman discovered the real reason Mordecai refused to bow, a fierce fire entered into his soul; all the hostilities and hatred of race were stirred into a flame; Haman resolved that Mordecai and his people will suffer.

Envy is not an isolated spirit; it has portrayed itself in every generation and in every society as the spirit of revenge. Christians have been the victims of revenge since the day of Pentecost; even within the Christian church, Christians have suffered. Under the Roman Caesars the Christians were treated as Haman intended to treat the Jews. Under a so-called Christian authority, whole communities were sacrificed to a retaliation which could not tolerate any sign of independent belief or action such as the Waldenses and other Protestants.

> *WALDENSES or Waldensians, Protestant religious group of medieval origin, called in French Vaudois. They originated in the late 12th cent. as the Poor Men of Lyons, a band organized by Peter Waldo, a wealthy merchant of Lyons, who gave away his*

property (c.1176) and went about preaching apostolic poverty as the way to perfection. Being laymen, they were forbidden to preach. They went to Rome, where Pope Alexander III blessed their life but forbade preaching (1179) without authorization from the local clergy. They disobeyed and began to teach unorthodox doctrines; they were formally declared heretics by Pope Lucius III in 1184 and by the Fourth Lateran Council in 1215. In 1211 more than 80 were burned as heretics at Strasbourg, beginning several centuries of persecution.

We need only to look at our present day prison system to see that spirits of envy and revenge are dominant factors in the fabric of our society. The wildest field on which the spirit of envy has poured out its venomous fury is not public; many families suffer from its outrageous affects. Mothers and fathers possessed with the spirit of envy have past down their envious personalities to their children who, if they were asked, really don't know why they dislike certain people. Personality is learned behavior and children easily adopt the behavior of their parents, without question. Envy promotes acts of sabotage that destroy the source of life for others. Let review Geneses 26:12-15

> *[12]Then Isaac sowed in that land, and received in the same year a hundredfold: and the LORD blessed him. [13]And the man waxed great, and went forward, and grew until he became very great: [14]for he had possession of flocks, and possession of herds, and great store of servants: and the Philistines envied him. [15]For all the wells which his father's servants had digged in the days of Abraham his father, the Philistines had stopped them, and filled them with earth. [16]And Abim'elech said unto Isaac, Go from us; for thou art much mightier than we.*

Abim'elech and the Philistines envied Isaac and his favor with God; water was the source of prosperity; without it there could be no fertilization of the fields, no reproduction of the cattle, and no yield of the fruit trees. Envy writes the songs that the enemy sings, "If I can't have it you shouldn't have it," but what God has for you, is for you. Between verses17 and 22 Isaac and his herdsman face insurmountable abuse of malice at the hands of the Philistines; they continually seize the possessions of Isaac and his families, but everywhere Isaac went he prospered. Not even the mightiest of enemies can sway the hand of God. The enemy may appear victorious and more prosperous than you, for awhile, but God only allows us to endure the chastisement of the wicket to test our faithfulness; you can rest assured that in due season we will come out more than conquerors.

And Isaac departed thence, and pitched his tent in the valley of Gerar, and dwelt there. ¹⁸And Isaac digged again the wells of water, which they had digged in the days of Abraham his father; for the Philistines had stopped them after the death of Abraham: and he called their names after the names by which his father had called them. ¹⁹And Isaac's servants digged in the valley, and found there a well of springing water. ²⁰And the herdmen of Gerar did strive with Isaac's herdmen, saying, The water is ours: and he called the name of the well Esek; because they strove with him. ²¹And they digged another well, and strove for that also: and he called the name of it Sitnah. ²²And he removed from thence, and digged another well; and for that they strove not: and he called the name of it Reho'both; and he said, For now the LORD hath made room for us, and we shall be fruitful in the land.

RESTORATION

W e have been dealing with conditioned hopelessness from the perspective of generational curses and how they may be passed down from one generation to the next, but Ezekiel after highlighting Israel's state of being, deals with hopelessness from the perspective of restoration. He notes that anyone can be put into or forced into a hopeless condition, cut off from his or her source of power and influence; he further infers that any believer or family, or community can find itself hopeless, cut off, abandoned to itself with nothing but misery and the prospect of destruction every day; it may be a castaway left on a lonely island to heal him or herself from the hurt of a relationship; it may be a condemned felon whose last effort to obtain a reprieve has failed, or a family left to perish in the inner city for a lack of food or shelter. Spiritually, there are those who are perplexed and distressed in their hearts because they cannot submit to the sound doctrine of the Church which separates truth from hypocrisy; others are hopeless because they cannot find the peace and rest they have long sought after.

There are those who feel hopeless because they have resolved that their sins are beyond forgiveness and their lives beyond restoration, mainly because they feel that no one cares for their souls or knows the depths of their extremity; they feel that everything and everyone has fail them, and that they are hopeless and must perish. When man fails us we can turn to God and trust Him; in Him the helpless and the hopeless find their refuge. Jesus said, "I am alone, and yet not alone, for the Father is with me". Many have found deliverance from their hopelessness where the Lord found them. It does not matter how low our condition of hopelessness may be, we can confidently count upon the near presence of God, His Divine and tender Mercy to deliver all who will submit to His Will.

Israel was enslaved in Egypt for 430 years to preserve the messianic bloodline; their condition seemed hopeless, but despite of their hopelessness they founded favor with God and were delivered. When we study the account of Israel's enslavement we see the circumstances of it as a part of God's predestined will, it was not because Israel had commit some great sin or due to any fault of her own. Some times God predestines purpose in our lives, and that purpose must be tried. Often the hopeless conditioning of a believer develops over time and not necessarily because of individual sin or generational curses or tradition or inherited habits.

In Ezekiel 37 the interpretation of the vision of the Valley of Dry Bones was given by the prophet himself; as it relates to the restoration of the people, Ezekiel wants us to be mindful of our hopelessness, but most of all marvel at God's Divine power of deliverance and Mercy. Like the Jews, many of us have endured the many profound afflictions and chastisements that have lead to the humiliation in which we have been plunged, and to us it seems more than just Divine commiseration. Restoration of the hopeless, the cast down, the out-caste, weak and weary must be orchestrated by the hand of God. "Behold I will open your graves, and cause you to come up out of your graves, O' my people" (Verse12). Some of our conditions were as if we were dead with them in our graves, but with God nothing is impossible; His voice can summon the dead from the grave to life as he did with Lazarus and the Shunammite woman's son. He can take your dire circumstances and turn them into a reality of hope.

The voice of restoration cries out from the depths of hopeless hearts; too often the hopeless sit speechless, unable to speak life into their own lives; but again remember, life and death are in the power of the tongue. If the hopeless would speak victory over themselves, restoration will take place. Joel Osteen writes, "Our words have creative power. With our words, we can either bless or curse our future. If you want to know what you're going to be like 5 years from now, listen to what you're saying about yourself; even the small things you say over your life from *"I'll never get that promotion"* to *"I'm just too tired all the time."* The moment we verbalize a thought, whether positive or negative, we give that thought the right to come to pass. To see God's best in your life, you have to stay on the offensive and speak victory over your life. The Bible says, *"Let the redeemed of the Lord say so."* It's not enough just to "not speak anything negative." You have to take it a step further and speak victory over your life. You can't speak defeat and expect to have victory. There is a correlation between what we say and what God does, but nothing happens until we speak our faith out. When we speak God's Word, the moment His promises come out of our mouth, something happens in the unseen realm. We may not see it for a week, a year or even ten years, but God is working behind the scene. If you keep saying the right thing, speaking victory, speaking favor, speaking health and wholeness the seeds you're sowing, you will reap. In due season, you will eat the fruit of your words, and God is going to make all your crooked places straight.

Hopeless conditions are like storms that toss and drive us to unseen perils and uncertain destines; they destroy us from within and ultimately from without; they make us see ourselves in the light of our struggle and not our destiny; we are forced to react according to our circumstances not according to our purpose. As it relates to speaking, we can turn pressure into power; we must realize that strange storms are only signs that we are close to victory and those old conquered strongholds and hidden weaknesses will be turned into abounding strength. Study the life of Jacob and other classic Bible characters and you will discover that the inner call of God will always outlast every external struggle. The horrific circumstances around us don't matter. God still has a plan for our lives!

Restoration is more than mending broken hearts and bringing closure to sad chapters in life; it is refusing to surrender to the will of the enemy; it is restoring wounded soldiers into Holy warfare for the glory of GOD. Although some may never be restored at their previous level of anointing, just finding a place to serve as a regenerated believer is worthy of eternal life. Failure among GOD'S people is nothing new; biblical history is littered with it. Samson failed. Abraham failed, Solomon failed, Jonah failed, The Hebrews failed, All twelve of the disciples of Jesus failed; Even King David, who was a man after GOD'S own heart, failed; in both Testaments, the evidence of failure is overwhelming but God's power of restoration is even the more sobering.

God's call for the fallen to return unto Him is a reoccurring theme throughout the scripture; it began with the call for individuals to renew their relationship with Him, then He called for groups of people, nations, and whole societies to repent and return to Him. As we study scripture we find that many of God's chosen drifted from the direction that He had purposed for them, but God, in due time, redirected their paths. We have to continue to read the scripture until we get to David before we hear the first cry for restoration. God withdrew His pleasures from David to force him to repentance of his sins. Although David, like many believers, never stopped loving God, he strayed away from the path of righteousness and had to be restored to a place in God where God could use him as a vestal of honor. Let's look at Samson, who allowed himself to be tempted by the flesh to stray from God's will; Samson's restoration came at his own request for physical strength to destroy his enemies; so his prayer was answered, he stepped into his purpose while at the same time meeting his own destiny, death.

Although it is better to die knowing that you have been restored into God Grace than to die in your sins; after reading this book it is my desire to see those who are out of the ark of safety be restored and given a second opportunity to work out their salvation with fear and trembling. All who hear the cry of God do not heed its call, such as the case with Ahab; God often sends warnings to the fallen, reminding them of His Divine Purpose, and when necessary, force them to return to Him. Ahab's sins, unlike David's, forced him deeper into his abomination against God. God's love and purpose for His people, for the Church, and the nation far more out weighs His concern for the personal aspirations and ambitions of any leader, no matter how popular or prestigious. The rod of correction comes from many directions: the voice of angels, the inspiration of a song, through prophecy sermons, through vision or inclination; it may come directly from the throne of God it self. Peter had several encounters where God put him back on the right road; "Whom He love He chastens" There was no other group of people more important to God's Divine plan of salvation than the Jews, Israel, His chosen people. There is no other group of people more important to God's Divine plan for the Church and eternal life today than the people of God, the baptized believer, the follower of the Lamb. Many have lost hope and feel that they are lost forever, but there is a remedy among those who are broken but still show up at prayer meeting; broken but still serve on the usher board, broken but still sing on the choir, broken, waiting for their day of reconciliation; waiting for believers like you and me, pastors and bishops to be the instrument that God uses to bring them back to a place in God where they can be used as a vestal of honor.

NOW FAITH IS

F aith is the substance of things hoped for, the evidence of things not seen. Our Faith connects us with God; without it, it is impossible to please Him; it is the assurance that God has not forgotten his promises to us, and the confidence that He will do just what he says, if we trust Him. Note in Deuteronomy 32:19-25 that God became displeased with Israel because it, as He put it, was a faithless people. Faith is often equated with or should I say though of as, the instrument by which we obtain things. The level of faith for the believer is beyond the acquisition of things; as believers, we don't need faith to obtain the physical or the materialistic, these are promised to us. *"I would that you prosper as your soul prospers."*

> *But without faith it is impossible to please him: for he that cometh to God must believe that he is, and that he is a rewarder of them that diligently seek him.*
>
> *Hebrews 11:6*

> *Beloved, I wish above all things that thou mayest prosper and be in health, even as thy soul prospereth.*
>
> *3 John 2*

> *If ye then be not able to do that thing which is least, why take ye thought for the rest? Consider the lilies how they grow: they toil not, they spin not; and yet I say unto you, that Solomon in*

*all his glory was not arrayed like one of these. If then God so
clothe the grass, which is to day in the field, and to morrow is
cast into the oven; how much more will he clothe you, O ye of
little faith? And seek not ye what ye shall eat, or what ye shall
drink, neither be ye of doubtful mind. For all these things do the
nations of the world seek after: and your Father knoweth that
ye have need of these things. But rather seek ye the kingdom of
God; and all these things shall be added unto you.*

Luke 12:26-31

Our faith is a spiritual gift for the development of our Christian
character; it places us on a higher plain in our relationship with God.
We are to use our faith to fortify our trust in God, to develop a stronger
willingness to submit to his Divine will. Now that we have become
conscious of the miraculous power of faith, it has presented us with a
paradox in understanding its awesomeness. To take full assurance of
its use we must fix the principles upon which we will use it. The first
principle to be decided is whether it is to be used to supply ones own
necessities which fulfills the physical cravings of the flesh.

*"Take no thought for your life either for the preservation of
it, if it be in danger, or for the provision that is to be made for
it, either of food or clothing, what ye shall eat or what ye shall
put on."*

Matthews 6:25

The paradox or the irony of have the knowledge of this power is that on
one side of the paradox is the carving to satisfy the bodily appetites and
carnal desires while on the other side is the divine sense of how to use
this new power. Human temptation through bodily cravings is the first
form that the enemy used; Eve in the garden, seeing that the three was
pleasant and good for food, surrendered to the will of the flesh. Men
have yielded to the appetites of the flesh from the beginning; the first

dilemma of man is that he is created with a carnal nature in which he is set to sustain his earthly relation. The members of the flesh should be the servant of man, but they are ever striving to be his master by seeking to secure its end by subtleties of craving and allurements.

The soul of man is of more value than the body; consider this, man is not a body; the truth of this statement is, that man has a body; a man's life is not in material things: eating, drinking, possessions; they only sustains his carnal nature. A man's real life consist in obedience to the will of God, as he may come to know it, and if that means starving the body or denying it, then the body must be starved or denied, and the Kingdom of God sought after.

We must pray that God's will be done; our faith must fall in line with God's will for our lives. When Jesus, in the book of Luke, was asked to do a miracle by demonstrating his power over the physical, to turn stones into bread, to jump from the pinnacle of the temple, or bow down an worship although to do any one of these miracles would have been easy, he did neither. Not one of the biblical characters asked for the physical when they were tested; their faith was always directed toward the fulfillment of God's will. In order for our faith to be an instrument of healing, we must focus on divine purpose and the predestined will of God; we must seek to be more obedient and to develop the fruit of the spirit in our lives.

Faith is the most import substance of the believer life; by it we are saved; we walk and are justified by it. Justification means that all charges of guilt, all acts of revenge, every instance of jealousy, of envy and strife are forgiven. Being justified by faith means that our brokenness of spirit, every generational curse, and hidden hurts have already been purchased by the redemptive blood of Jesus; by His scripts we are healed.

www.ingramcontent.com/pod-product-compliance
Lightning Source LLC
Chambersburg PA
CBHW031448120626
46545CB00006B/2613